Beyond Conventional Boundaries

STUDIES IN INCLUSIVE EDUCATION
Volume 13

Scope
This series addresses the many different forms of exclusion that occur in schooling across a range of international contexts and considers strategies for increasing the inclusion and success of all students. In many school jurisdictions the most reliable predictors of educational failure include poverty, Aboriginality and disability. Traditionally schools have not been pressed to deal with exclusion and failure. Failing students were blamed for their lack of attainment and were either placed in segregated educational settings or encouraged to leave and enter the unskilled labour market. The crisis in the labor market and the call by parents for the inclusion of their children in their neighborhood school has made visible the failure of schools to include all children.

Drawing from a range of researchers and educators from around the world, Studies in Inclusive Education will demonstrate the ways in which schools contribute to the failure of different student identities on the basis of gender, race, language, sexuality, disability, socio-economic status and geographic isolation. This series differs from existing work in inclusive education by expanding the focus from a narrow consideration of what has been traditionally referred to as special educational needs to understand school failure and exclusion in all its forms. Moreover, the series will consider exclusion and inclusion across all sectors of education: early years, elementary and secondary schooling, and higher education.

Beyond Conventional Boundaries

Uncertainty in Research and Practice with Children

Daniela Mercieca

SENSE PUBLISHERS
ROTTERDAM/BOSTON/TAIPEI

A C.I.P. record for this book is available from the Library of Congress.

ISBN: 978-94-6091-488-1 (paperback)
ISBN: 978-94-6091-489-8 (hardback)
ISBN: 978-94-6091-490-4 (e-book)

Published by: Sense Publishers,
P.O. Box 21858,
3001 AW Rotterdam,
The Netherlands
www.sensepublishers.com

Printed on acid-free paper

DEDICATION

This book is dedicated to my parents Catherine and Winston with love

TABLE OF CONTENTS

CHAPTER 1

POSTSCRIPT

This is a book about how 'uncertainty' can be viewed differently when carrying out research and also in professional practice. It gives an account of the process which I went through to experience this uncertainty, highlighting the various theories, encounters and reflections which led to it. Originally a work which led to the awarding of a PhD, three years down the road, the focus of this book is now for professionals working with children, as well as for research with children. The standard methods of research, which I yearned for, were proving more and more inadequate for what it was that I wanted to write about. It was in fact quite a liberating experience to take a different approach, albeit a rather frightening one. As explained further in the book, the hardship lay in feeling lost for quite a while, and also in eventually needing to 'cover' myself and my choices – one cannot drift away from the straight and narrow paths without adequate justification and foundation.

This first chapter is presented as a postscript, with tensions and thoughts laid out in hindsight. Thus this chapter is a form of meta-writing, exposing the meanderings of the process and providing the reader with an account of the style of the writing, the content, the arguments and also the manner in which these were tackled. The title emerged from the process of writing the rest of the work and is a summing up of the points explored, rather than simply an introduction to them. This is also because the subject of the book is the result of a process. I approached the doctorate assuming that a fixed idea of its subject was needed. However, the interesting prospect of an alternative route was offered, which in retrospect had more to do with an understanding of psychoanalytic processes as explained below. Unlike conventional research, the approach to the doctorate was to allow time and space for the ideas which I was engaged with to emerge in the form of functional statements. Melanie Klein (1997) highlights conflict as important for the future stability of the ego. A balance needs to be reached which is however very delicate and which is upset at every little challenge, following which, balance is aimed at once more. This is the process which I now, in hindsight, understand constituted the initial stages of my research. In a state of suspension, I felt very vulnerable and confused with minor moments of stability, which, however, were still felt as steps moving forward.

> Feelings can be and often are *revelations* of the state of life within the entire organism – a lifting of the veil in the literal sense of the term. Life being a high-wire act, most feelings are expressions of the struggle for balance, ideas of the exquisite adjustments and corrections without which, one mistake too many, the whole act collapses. (Damasio, 2004, p. 6, author's emphasis).

I find it necessary to locate this book in a temporal context. Having just graduated from my professional training when I started this research, while struggling with it,

I was also getting to grips with a new role in a new profession. What thus connected both my studies and my practice was the need to cope with an increasing feeling of inadequacy and a difficulty to remain afloat in both. Now I realise that these events provided me with the rare opportunity to reflect and focus on myself. The aforementioned balance which is vital for stability was very much shaken and through the spiralling process of instability and stability emerged a continuous discovery. This took the form of literature read, children and families worked with, the different contexts in which the practices took place, strengths and vulnerabilities of the self and an interaction of all these within the research and the developing practice. Inadvertently then, the research and the practice developed together, as I could not ignore any aspect of either. What eventually ensued, however, was that the research and practice became in themselves targets of reflection through the realisation that my concerns were about something larger than myself. I thought less about my anxiety in dealing with the research and focused on ideas which provided opportunities for the research being different. In my practice, I allowed myself not to know and thus came to the possibility of perceiving practice differently. My perspective thus widened, moving from fears of inadequacy to gaining confidence in the profession and the research.

This is also reflected in this writing. Throughout I engage with the literature mentioned above. I use three main stories of my involvement with children, which stories I then use to highlight the ethical implications and dilemmas inherent in practice. Besides this however, I also write about myself as caught up in the aforementioned process as part of the 'data' of the research. These particular constituents of this book are intertwined throughout as the stories of my work with particular children, the context in which they take place, my own self-growth in research and practice, the literature, and the implications which all have on the profession, contribute to the book. I do not call this writing the end product because I firmly argue that I am not arriving at the end of a journey, but see this as an opportunity to pause for a while and write about my thoughts and arguments as they are at the time being. The ramifications and implications of my arguments about the practice of helping professions make the issue bigger than myself and deserve their space in the book.

Feeling elated that I had reached my long-awaited aim of becoming an educational psychologist, I wrote about my hopes and aspirations in my journal. A recurring theme emerged, which rotated around my horror at the realisation of the implications of my role and my ensuing fears. Although I had understood that my role in working with children was quite an influential one, it took time to come to terms with an acknowledgement of the responsibilities which I felt I was carrying. I explored these in what was becoming a journal which was confronted with various readings. I began to think that I was going on a long journey of self-exploration. Was this writing about self-searching as a person, as a psychologist, both? As yet I was not clear and did not have the research questions, neither did I have, or seemed to be planning to have, any data worth analysing.

However, I started to see that what I was uneasy about, and what intrigued me, were the various tensions which I was experiencing in my work. Now the latter phrase of that sentence is the kernel of one of the tensions. There is the *I* and there is also the *work*, and the words *was experiencing in* imply that the two had to have some kind of relationship with each other. In this work,

> the question is not how to separate the subject from the object as much as possible, for subject and object are inseparable. 'I' and 'world' … are inextricably entwined. The I makes meaning and can do no differently. It is logically impossible to detach the I from the world. It is no use asking for a world without I, if only because the search for a world without I already presupposes an I. (Levering, 2006, p. 451)

This issue is tackled further throughout the book but it should here suffice to explain that the subject of this book started with my practice with children, the children themselves, and has now been expanded to address the profession of the educational psychologist itself and also other helping professionals working with children. Thus, all are very much included in the book in that some experiences of my own training and practice are recounted and the issues raised from such anecdotes are discussed in relation to the profession of an educational psychologist and that of other helping professionals. All three strands are somewhat intertwined as I constantly move from the self, to the children, to the profession and back in a reflexive manner, trying to show how each influences the other. Here again the focus is on the aim of finding the right balance. Eventually a statement which I felt I could work with emerged. The book concerns ethical dilemmas which the person in the practitioner's role encounters. The balance itself is an ethical exercise, just as everything else one does is ethical (this is a loaded statement and will be expanded further in Chapter 3). Thus, the ethical dilemmas written about in this book are relevant both to the research process as well as the practice.

One of the recurrent difficulties was my position in the writing. At its simplest this raises the issue of whether to write using the first person or whether to adopt the passive form of sentence construction. The latter may be seen as more objective, "looking only at the facts, setting aside personal preference or interest. In this context a sense of something shameful, or at least weak, attaches to subjective" (Williams, 1976, p. 312). However, as argued above, the subjective is an inevitable starting point in this book. In no way do I want to remove agency by using the passive voice, although there are instances in the writing where the passive voice is useful as a way of sharing responsibility for something rather than positioning that responsibility outside my colleagues and myself. I also use the first person singular and plural as readers are positioned as allies whose thoughts I hope will resonate with the perspectives discussed. As Hyatt (2006) mentions, the use of the first person pronoun assumes shared knowledge, beliefs and values, so that although "as I write, I have a sense of me, and… as you read, you have a sense of you" (Damasio, 1999, p. 10), still both are assumed to have a shared understanding.

Chapter 4 starts by questioning the style of writing that is used in the book. Issues concerning the writing style also rotated around the character which I was to adopt. Further on, I try to make a case for the virtuous practitioner who is constantly trying to better herself. Am I thus claiming that I am such a practitioner? At times I found myself facing such a question and recoiled from it with disgust. The implications were frightening because of their possible closeness to my perception of myself and my profession. How could I dismiss this question without seeming to run away from it? For the fact that this issue is so significant implies that it is important to me. I do give a lot of importance to whether I feel that I have acted in the best way that I possibly can in my work with children. From that position, it is difficult to refrain from having my own thoughts about the actions of other practitioners. Sometimes I have admiration for the way other professionals handle situations. On the other hand, I sometimes feel that I would have tried to act otherwise. How can I write about this without being judgemental, or worse, self-righteous, and thus losing virtue?

I found an expression of this in a beautiful quotation of Standish (2004), who outlines the virtuous person as one who never feels she has done enough and "who has some sense of the infinite possibilities of her relation to the other" (p. 494). I find it very apt for this situation because it implies that the virtuous person is one who does not feel or think virtuous. I did not want to write about myself as some kind of saviour of children with various needs. Neither was I willing to write a book which featured me or other practitioners as villains of a story. Some situations I experienced in my practice also tempted me to regard myself as a martyr sacrificed in the cause of children, but I was not comfortable in the role and disliked the tenor of such writing. A different understanding of the situations which I was experiencing was needed and this slowly emerged with the help of the doctorate supervision which I received and also with different opportunities to look at the work of an educational psychologist. Thus although I do write about my own formation and experiences with children, the focus is on the larger picture than me either as a person or as a practitioner. The issue is politicised through the movement from the particular to the general. The book concerns the profession of educational psychology and other helping professions such as social work, teachers, and counsellors and their future in a political and economic context, which context seems to go against what they stand for. It is relevant for all practitioners as the political and ethical implications are highlighted. I expand on this in Chapters 7 and 8.

Some chance encounters with philosophers encouraged me in my interest. I recently received some enigmatic feedback about my views from the person who first taught me philosophy at sixth form, who said that they would make a philosopher of me yet. I was puzzled as I had always thought that my questions were those of any psychologist and that the discussions surrounding such questions were fixed in the realm of psychology and central to its nature. In fact I took umbrage when a colleague once told me that my thesis seemed very philosophical as I perceived that the implication was that it was removed from the practical. The realisation came later, as I read the works of philosophers of education – owing perhaps to the nature of work and the institutions where psychologists work, it is difficult to come across more than a few psychologists who address these questions, so that these are thus deemed philosophical in nature. Unfortunately, we succumb to the pressures of today's fast and ever-changing world and may forget to revisit some fundamental tenets of our practice.

Thus, I resorted to reading journals and attending conferences on philosophy of education to understand more about questions and issues which I have always thought were deeply psychological. Although conscious efforts were made to resist compartmentalisation and classification of thoughts, I realised that I used to consider the realm of emotion as solely psychological. Coming across Spinoza (1989) I realised I was in error, as I read about the interaction of rationality and emotion in such a way that it forcibly reminded me of previous readings of Bion (1994) and Klein (1997), both of whom were pioneering psychoanalysts and whom I introduce later in this chapter. With this encouragement to nullify boundaries between disciplines, the philosophical trail was pursued. Winch's (1990) statement that sociology was a disguised form of philosophy gave some indication that my predicament was not isolated and strengthened my belief that if I ignored the philosophical I would be impoverishing the psychological in this work. "...to be clear about the nature of philosophy and to be clear about the nature of the social studies amount to the same thing. For any worthwhile study of society must be philosophical in character and any worthwhile philosophy must be concerned with the nature of human society" (Winch, 1990, p. 3).

A different kind of reading was called for, one in which I had to learn that I could not expect to instantly understand what I was reading. Several readings of a text were required, and my understanding gradually improved with the passing of time. Indeed, my attendance of some philosophy lectures and conferences taught me that eminent philosophers still disagree among themselves about the meanings and interpretations of some texts. I was comforted when I read others who had similar experiences of reading texts: when Damasio (2004) returned to Spinoza as a professional adult after first reading Ethics as an adolescent, he discovered that "Spinoza was still the same, but [he] was not" (p. 10). Even now, as I am finalising this writing, I revert back to quotations and find myself re-reading chapters and gaining a qualitatively different understanding of texts, besides having a feeling that I have understood more of them. It is a continuous process – in the same way that I feel that as long as I continue to revise this writing, my ideas will evolve further and I feel the urge to change what is written. The numerous readings of a text bring about different understandings of it, as the evolved self interacts with the text each time.

Thus, in this writing I call on philosophers for support for my thoughts and questions. An important source of ideas is Alasdair MacIntyre, particularly his book After Virtue (2000), as he writes about good being defined by practice. This writing is of interest to me as I am focusing on the helping professions and on the qualities required by the practitioner who is aiming to fulfil her potential through working with children. Paul Standish's (2001) work urged me to question that which is taken for granted, whether in research or in practice. Furthermore, Standish (2002b, 2004, 2005b) writes about the difficulties which practices encounter owing to the changing nature of organisation and management of institutions. Jon Nixon's work (2001a, 2003, 2004b; Nixon et al., 1997; Nixon and Walker 2004) rotates also around this issue with particular reference to MacIntyre's (2000) writing.

It was interesting to locate the study of emotions also in contemporary neuroscience. Damasio (1999) writes profusely about emotion, although he says that throughout most of the twentieth century, emotion was not trusted in the laboratory. He finds that Charles Darwin, William James and Sigmund Freud have written extensively about emotion and given it a privileged place in scientific discourse, but this was not developed.

> Emotion was too subjective, it was said. Emotion was too elusive and vague. Emotion was at the opposite end from reason, easily the finest human ability, and reason was presumed to be entirely independent from emotion. This was a perverse twist on the Romantic view of humanity. Romantics placed emotion in the body and reason in the brain. Twentieth-century science left out the body, moved emotion back into the brain, but relegated it to the lower neural strata associated with ancestors who no one worshipped. In the end, not only was emotion not rational, even studying it was probably not rational (Damasio, 1999, p. 39).

Yet within neuroscience and within philosophy it can be seen that emotion can be systematically studied and given a prominent place when viewed in terms of its interdependent relationship with reason, learning and growth.

I was also introduced to psychoanalytical literature on the basis that similar questions might arise from a very different perspective. Once more I experienced the frustration of finding the literature very difficult to engage with. An adaptation in my attitude towards reading was again required, and I found myself preferring to read less widely but to make what I read my own, especially with psychoanalytical writing. I read some of Melanie Klein's (1997) writing, particularly where it concerns the process of splitting. I related it to my own work because of Hollway's (1994) and Hollway and Jefferson's (2001) work when they write about defended subjects and also about the sense of self which is non-unitary. The possibility of viewing people as in a constant process as opposed to perceiving them as fixed gave me many opportunities and provided me with a language to express my own thoughts on the subject in relation to our practice and ourselves. Wilfred Bion (1994), another psychoanalyst, provided me with an explanation of my own difficulties handling my emotional responses, which responses I perceived as interfering with my work. The interdependence of emotion and reason as outlined by Bion (1994) allows me to relate my experience to the profession at large. I resort to Bion (1994) to write about uncertainty in terms which are not negative but which may even describe uncertainty as a necessary and important state of being in the work of the educational psychologist with children.

Thus both philosophy and psychoanalysis provide me with theory with which to develop my view of the practitioner as in a constant state of becoming. I therefore move to and from both kinds of literature without delineating fixed boundaries between the two. The two readings allow a richer and fuller expression of my arguments.

STRUCTURE OF BOOK

In this introductory chapter the constituting elements of this book are outlined and the links between them defined. An explanation as to how these emerged from the literature is also given in this chapter. Chapter 2 outlines reasons for my pursuing research in this manner. This part of the book was found to be increasingly important as the need was felt to explain why the process seemed so messy, and why I seemed unwilling or unable to do away with the mess. An introduction of the issues which are investigated ensues in Chapter 3 as a necessary prerequisite to finding "the proper unit of study" (Newman and Holzman, 1993, p. 22, in Billington, 2000, p. 73). The chapter starts with a discussion of ethics in the practice of educational psychology; this discussion inquires whether codes of ethics suffice for helping professionals. The context put forward is the practice of working with children as imbued with ethics and ethical dilemmas which practitioners may or may not be aware of. One of the questions posed is whether knowledge of facts and written procedures and policies can substitute the practitioner's judgement. This question is then located in the context of today's world with its fast pace and requirement for order and precision. Both philosophical and psychoanalytic literature is used as the defended individual is placed in this context. The final question addressed in this chapter concerns the becoming of educational psychologists and their profession. Starting from the self, the argument then shifts onto the practice of educational psychology using some ideas from MacIntyre (2000).

Chapter 4 is the first of three chapters which rotate around the theme of dilemmas in uncertainty. The main focus of this chapter is on the research process. I write about my own research experiences and relate them to the research process of the doctorate, where the complexity of what is explored is reflected in the complexity of the research method. Issues of the nature of scientific research are raised with a view to inquiring whether this research is far removed from systematic inquiry. While previously wondering whether my uncertainty was the result of incompetence, I now argue that it is important for the researcher to feel suspended in uncertainty before latching onto a research design. The phase of circumspection mentioned by Bannister (1981 in Mellor 1998) is given worth as part of the creative process of research. There is a parallel writing of uncertainty in my research and in my practice, which culminates in the story of Geoffrey in Chapter 5. The argument is thus taken further through the exposition of two accounts of my own progress as a practitioner in general and in particular with Geoffrey. They serve to contextualise the issues of uncertainty and anxiety in practice; the narratives reflect the search for certainty and validation of self in the educational psychologist working with children. Geoffrey is a boy of primary school age who was referred by his parents for an assessment. The literature mentioned in the previous chapter and my entries in my research journal are further used to analyse my work with Geoffrey and his family. How does the practitioner manage to contain the anxiety which uncertainty creates? Is it just a question of knowing more facts? Through the reading of authors like Bion (1994), Billington (2000), and Damasio (1999), Chapter 6 explores how uncertainty and anxiety can be turned to good use rather than being a debilitating force to the practising psychologist.

The second theme of the book concerns dilemmas in professional issues. Chapter 7 starts by asking for a definition of the work of an educational psychologist leading to the question of how this work is to be evaluated. I suggest that the work of the educational psychologist is to bring about the best welfare of the particular child that one is working with. However, considering the professional and personal bifurcation of the social world, I argue that there is a fundamental contradiction when the professional psychologist interacts with the private life of the child and family. When sharing these concerns, I was told that these issues can and ought to be dealt with in therapy and/or supervision. However, the aim here is not to deal with these issues and have them settled. Rather the intention is to investigate what they are based on and whether they ought to be considered as issues which should be settled one way or another. The story of Gemma in Chapter 8 is used to bring out examples of difficulties in the ethics of practice with these ideas, also using my own reflections on this case and the literature as data. Nagel's (2002) fragmentation of value is applied to the story in this chapter, questioning whether one can decide with any finality which of his five sources of value is to have most weight in any one decision.

The theme around which the last three chapters of the book rotate is dilemmas and virtues. Chapter 9 starts with an outline of the context of the story of Alexandra and my involvement with her and her mother. Similarly, in this child's story as with the previous two, there is great anxiety over the practitioner's role in this child's well-being. The awareness of responsibility which comes with the profession is overwhelming, as is the story of Alexandra's life as recounted by her mother. Practitioners may find themselves in situations where institutional expediency overrides other considerations. Should the practitioner blindly follow procedure or should the circumstances of the case which the practitioner faces lead to a judgement where procedure is not followed? Chapter 10 discusses the difficulties of keeping children first and foremost in one's mind in the light of other claims on the psychologist's time, touching upon issues of performativity, accountability and efficiency. An attempt to remove responsibility (or perhaps to ensure that everyone's actions can be accounted for and regulated) can be seen in the formulation of policies and procedures which are expected to be followed. However, these do not remove the 'buts' from the mind of the practitioner whose judgement sometimes goes against the policy followed by the institution where the practitioner works. Chapter 11 concerns the judgement and virtues of the educational psychologist using MacIntyre (2000), Smith (2003, 2006), Standish (1997, 2001, 2004, 2005b) and Nixon (2001a; Nixon and Walker, 2004) to help with the exploration of these questions. This chapter also draws together the arguments and suggests the application of these in formation of helping professionals.

CHAPTER 2

MAKING SENSE OF THE PROCESS

This chapter explains the manner in which ethical dilemmas in the practice of educational psychology and other helping professions were tackled for the purposes of this research. How does one research ethical dilemmas? Although my initial intentions were to follow on previous research experiences, the complexity of method started to dawn on me. Smith makes a link between the Baconian tradition that "business be done as if by machinery" (Ellis and Spedding (trans.) in Robertson, (1905) in Smith, 2006, p. 157) and "the [prevailing] notion that there exist research methods that can be acquired relatively straightforwardly by almost any aspiring researcher, irrespective of his or her general intellectual sophistication, quality of judgement and understanding of the subject being researched" (ibid., p. 160).

Perhaps the easier way of tackling this question is to start from the methodologies which would definitely not serve the purpose, and in so doing, to give a better definition of the methodology that was adopted. The nature of the topic might automatically exclude quantitative methodology. Could some form of questionnaire be administered with tick-boxes, or even one with open-ended questions, with the aim of starting a discussion and exploration of these dilemmatic situations? Is objectivity, as distinct from subjectivity, aimed for here? Williams (1976) describes the former as having the sense of being

> factual, fair-minded (neutral) and hence reliable, as distinct from the sense of subjective as based on impressions rather than facts, and hence influenced by personal feelings and thus being relatively unreliable. There can be no doubt where these senses come from. They are from the procedures of Positivist Science and from the associated social, political and administrative senses of 'impartial' and 'neutral' judgement (p. 311).

However, as mentioned in Chapter 1, the subjective is given importance here, as the starting point from which further ethical and political statements about the profession are made. Thus, a qualitative approach is called for. "To understand an educational practice requires the careful analysis of the social situation – the underlying social rules, the interpretation of the participants, the values and aims embedded within the practice. Such 'qualitative research' is quite clearly necessary…" (Pring, 2000, p. 258). Parker (2005) suggests that the reason for which qualitative research in psychology has concerns about mainstream quantitative approaches "is not because quantification is wrong, but because psychologists often do quantitative research so badly" (p. 9). Many of the issues rotate around the question of causality, in that the question is asked whether prediction has a place in the social sciences.

> Given that we cannot predict the future even in the presence of our best causal investigations does the mode of explanation really matter? Must indeterminism

> lead to indifference? Is it the conclusion that, though we may not live in a deterministic universe, the best we can aim for is the identification of necessary or sufficient conditions, for causal processes and statistical regularity? (Smeyers, 2001, p. 488).

In this research, neither causality nor prediction is sought. In essence the hypothesis is: there is a mess – now how can it be explored and written about systematically?

> If much of the world is vague, diffuse or unspecific, slippery, emotional, ephermeral, elusive or indistinct, changes like a kaleidoscope, or doesn't really have much of a pattern at all, then where does this leave social science? How might we catch some of the realities we are currently missing? Can we know them well? *Should* we know them? Is 'knowing' the metaphor that we need? And if it isn't, then how might we relate to them? (Law, 2006, p. 2).

This writing aims to bring together the practitioner, the children, the respective pressures on both in their daily lives, as well as the dilemmatic situations to which they contribute. These situations in a contingent world cannot be adequately represented in a simple and straightforward way. How might it be possible to convey to readers this complexity and mess in a systematic way – can this amalgamation of events, circumstances, beings and actions be contained within the writing so that those who read it grasp the message which is portrayed? It is an impossible task but one which has tantalised social science.

When carrying out research, one is expected to follow some method, even if the limitations of that method are outlined towards the end. I had already eliminated questionnaires. Could I then observe a few practitioners in their work and see whether and how they tackled the ethical issues which they faced on a daily basis? This was also not helpful because it was not a question of actions which I could observe. The situations which make practitioners uncomfortable may not come out in the open but may take the form of thoughts, sometimes even vague ones. I originally attempted to carry out interviews of a few chosen practitioners, hoping to be able to use them as data. The result of this exercise was that it helped me to raise more questions about what it was that I was researching. These questions are explored in Chapter 4. I started to agree with Law (2006) that "while standard methods are often extremely good at what they do, they are badly adapted to the study of the ephemeral, the indefinite and the irregular....this implies that the problem is not so much the standard research methods themselves, but the normatives that are attached to them in discourses about method" (p. 4).

I had already started keeping a journal of my thoughts and feelings as resulting from my interaction with children, particularly those I met as a practitioner. In this journal I explored both my stories of the children and their families and my involvement in them. I questioned my role and those of other professionals and I also questioned the different outcomes of my interaction, such as the ways in which I wrote about children. I would take the journal to my supervisor during tutorials and on the basis on what was written, he would recommend authors whom I could read to help me explore the issues I mentioned. Needless to say, the "I" started to take an increasingly prominent position in my writing and I found that perhaps the best, although still, I believe, inadequate, way of representing these situations was to convey my experience of them and to problematise such experience.

This seems to start having a resemblance to action research, as "in action research the research 'question' arises out of the problems of practitioners and it is an important aspect of this approach that the analysis of the situation is *in situ*" (Banister et al., 1995, p. 110). However, the main focus of action research is on the effects of changes applied to a social situation: "the immediate aim of the research is to understand these problems, and the researcher, who may or may not be the actual practitioner, formulates speculative and tentative general principles about the problems that have been identified. From these it is possible to generate hypotheses about what action is likely to lead to (desired) improvements. The action can then be tried out and data on its effect collected, and the data can then be used to revise the earlier hypothesis" (ibid.). This did not appear to me to be what I was aiming to do. Carr (2006), however, uses Aristotle and Gadamar in order to argue that "our conception of action research as a form of methodologically principled social scientific inquiry has been contaminated by the prejudices of modernity and ... these prejudices continue to exercise a distorting influence on the way in which action research is now conducted and understood" (p. 432). He further claims that the action research paradigm has rendered practical philosophy obsolete, so that "the philosophical analysis of the role of human reason in the development of practical knowledge" (p. 432) was replaced by the need to develop a research methodology which allowed for the scientific study of action. In this way, by embracing the notion of methodology, action research could have a place for itself within the prejudices of the dominant culture of modernity. "But in doing this, action research itself became deeply implicated in depriving *praxis* of the tradition of inquiry through which it had hitherto been articulated and sustained" (p. 432). In Carr's explanation, it does seem as though my research fits in his understanding of action research which focuses on its historical development. Carr (2006) makes certain provisos for this to take place as can be read in the following:

> However, once action research is prepared to expand its own 'historical horizons' – once, that is, it is prepared to make its own implicit acceptance of the dominant beliefs of modernity explicit – then it should become increasingly apparent why action research can only be made intelligible as a mode of inquiry that aspires to create and nurture the kind of dialogical communities within which *phronesis* can be embedded and which the development of *praxis* presupposes and requires. If it were to be understood in this way, action research would no longer feel it necessary to demonstrate its legitimacy by appealing to a methodology....
>
> ...Action research would no longer be understood as a social science 'research paradigm' that can achieve what conventional social scientific research has conspicuously failed to achieve. Rather it would be regarded as nothing other than a post-modern manifestation of the pre-modern Aristotelian tradition of practical philosophy (Carr, 2006, p. 433).

This is similar to what I have attempted to carry out here, a questioning of the givens in the work of professionals with children with a view towards a better awareness of where such assumptions come from and whether they aid or hinder practice. The ultimate aim is that of having such questioning included more necessarily and firmly within our profession.

Thus, besides using my journal where I wrote about particular children, I also used the case notes and reports of the children which I mention. These were a rich source of data and, I found, as I go back to them, that I was transported to those thoughts and emotions as experienced then. However, the experiences started to form part of a bigger picture. I thus also wrote about my personal experiences as relevant to the issues I explore. These experiences include my involvement with research, my own professional training and the situations I came in contact with at my work place.

The readings which I delved into are not simply used to validate the journal and stories of my involvement with the children. The literature forms part of my data as it provokes and forms the question of dilemmas, centring on the work of the helping professionals and the educational psychologist in particular. In the different sections, the literature is developed alongside the stories and the problems that these stories divulge. Most of the readings I have engaged with are written by psychologists and philosophers in the area of education and I was increasingly drawn to the perspective of psychology which is philosophical in nature. While sympathetic with Winch (1990) when he says that the social sciences are but a disguised form of philosophy, I would previously have claimed that my questions are deeply psychological and even now I am not sure that I would have been incorrect in my view. Either way, no research in social science can do away with its ethical implications – research is not neutral and contributes to the political and ethical aspects of human life. Law (2006) insists "that methods, their rules, and even more methods' practices not only describe but also help *produce* the reality that they understand" (Law, 2006, p. 5). Thus he argues that, since methods inescapably shape the world, let us acknowledge this process and work within it.

> I am not recommending political quietism.... Since social (and natural) science investigations interfere with the world, in one way or another they always make a difference, politically and otherwise. Things change as a result. The issue, then, is not to seek disengagement but rather with how to engage. It is about how to make good differences in circumstances where reality is both unknowable and generative (Law, 2006, p. 7).

Standish (2001) writes about "the examiner's dismay" when the latter does not manage to locate the expected sections in a student's thesis. Does this mean that the research lacks rigour? Has the student not been advised and supervised properly? These are all questions which I was asked by concerned friends and colleagues. Where is the separation between means and ends? The thing is I feel that I now do not really know these separations and sections. I had always found them to be very useful because they structure the work which seems like a tangled ball of string. I had, on previous occasions, written dissertations with these divisors (this point will be expanded further in Chapter 4). I believe, however, that this writing needs to work with its entanglement because any disentanglement would result in an over-simplification of it, to the extent that it would be modified beyond recognition.

It would be very easy to succumb to the temptation to iron away or suppress contradictions in my accounts and that would defeat the whole purpose. "To grasp a person through the 'whole' of what we know about him or her does not have to imply that he or she is consistent, coherent or rational" (Hollway and Jefferson, 2001, p. 70). The separations and sections are, I believe, 'givens' (Standish, 2001) which I do not find useful.

This 'method', if such it can be called, this attempt to question 'givens' in the writing of the research, reflects the attempt to question 'givens' in my work as a practitioner with children. I want to question my practice in that I am trying to uncover the layers beneath assumptions which practitioners work with. Quoting Tickle (2001), it seems that I am opening windows on the practice of helping professionals, which action he calls "an action research disposition towards my work ... as a means of increasing our capacity for practical wisdom" (Tickle, 2001, p. 348). I write about dilemmas, ethics and moral purposefulness: as Standish (2001) claims, "values permeate our lives and ... the ethical is in some sense prior" (p. 487). Thus, in the same way that I am systematically critiquing and exploring the possibilities of further development of the practice of the helping professions, on ethical grounds, I am also questioning the given or 'normal' way of presenting my research because I believe that it would diminish what I want to do. It is particularly difficult to avoid using the phrases 'writing up', 'represent' and other words which easily spring to mind as I write about it.

Williams (1976) explores the history of the word 'science' and writes that in the later sixteenth century, the word 'scientific' meant a theoretical or demonstrative proof of an argument. In the early eighteenth century, moreover, 'science' was applied to the use of arguments or propositions to explore any subject – the term was applied to the process rather than to the content. "The meaning that was thus coming through, from the whole body of learning, had elements both of method and of demonstration, at a theoretical level; science was a kind of knowledge or argument, rather than a kind of subject" (1976, p. 277). Thus, although my enquiry in this research is not standard in that one would not find it listed under 'methods' in textbooks, this is purposefully so because I want to engage with what Law terms as "complex, diffuse and messy" (Law, 2006, p. 2). This is not "a way of saying that 'anything goes' and one can believe what one wants" (ibid., p. 13), but is a systematic enquiry into the professional practice of educational psychologists and other helping professionals. I expand on this further in Chapter 4, where the importance of knowing is questioned. Knowledge and method do not evolve in a vacuum but "participate in the social world, being shaped *by* it, and simultaneously *shaping* it" (ibid., p. 12). The work of the educational psychologist involves herself working with children and families, not to mention the significant others in schools. This scenario is a complex one and thus "(social) sciences should also be trying to make and know realities that are vague and indefinite *because much of the world is enacted in that way*" (ibid., p. 14).

THE STORIES

Although this is completely coincidental, the three children whom I write about in the previously-mentioned chapters come from different aspects of my experience in practice. I would like to emphasise that the significance of the children chosen is not a property of the cases which they presented but the work that I put them to (Hollway, 1994, p. 36). They were chosen with a purpose in mind: that of making their stories work for me. These stories are my representations of them. I was an actor in these stories myself and I decided to use these stories for my research only after my involvement with these children. The reason why I chose these was that while I worked with these children I was very conscious of the ethical and political implications of my every movement and thought. As Walkerdine puts it, '[the fact] that the feelings came up in me told me something … that I wanted to take as data' (1997:67)" (in Hollway, 1994, p. 45).

CONCLUSION

> Method? What we're dealing with here is not, of course, just method. It is not just a set of techniques. It is not just a philosophy of method, a methodology. It is not even simply about the kinds of realities that we want to recognise or the kinds of worlds we might hope to make. It is also, and most fundamentally about a way of being. It is about what kinds of social sciences we want to practice. And then, and as a part of this, it is about the kinds of people that we want to be, and about how we should live (Addleson, 1994). Method goes with work, and ways of working, and ways of being.... To live more in and through slow method, or vulnerable method, or quiet method. Multiple method. Modest method. Uncertain method. Diverse method (Law, 2006, p. 10–11).

Law's words express what I am trying to achieve in the following chapters. The method of research which is used, as well as my professional practice, reflects and influences a process of becoming. The writing is becoming deployed, the author and the concepts used in it are too and so, applying the same logic, is the reader. Thus, both the manner in which the research was carried out as well as the content, contribute originally to knowledge. Different disciplines are used to question practice on issues, which issues emerge following a systematic exploration of a subjective experience with children. There are several aspects explored: research and practice; the overlapping nature of philosophy and psychology, which incorporates both neuroscience and psychoanalysis; the personal and the professional. The profession of the caring professional is an excellent site for the exploration of these aspects, particularly as the nature of the practice is set in a political and ethical context owing to the variety of institutions that the professional works with and within on a daily basis.

CHAPTER 3

ETHICAL DILEMMAS

This chapter consists of a lengthy introduction, in which I describe the complexity of the topic. The subject of the book is explored, drawing on the various arguments put forward in later chapters. It is important that these arguments are introduced here as they both form part of, and also lead towards, the unit of study which is ethical dilemmas. This approach resembles Billig et al.'s (1988), who call it "a discursive travelogue which offers reasons why one path and not another can be recommended and what views can be expected by travellers along the way" (p. 8) and contrast it to "the simple map reference" (ibid.), which may be more precise, but possibly less helpful.

I discuss issues of dilemmas and ethics and put them in the context of the profession, the practitioner as a person and also society at large. The chapter starts with a discussion of ethics in the practice of educational psychology, with an enquiry on whether practitioners can feel that codes of ethics provide the last word on ethical questions they meet on a daily basis in their work. One of the questions posed is whether knowledge of facts and written procedures and policies can substitute the practitioner's judgement. This question is then located in the context of today's world with its fast pace and requirement for order and precision. Both philosophical and psychoanalytic literature is used as the uncertain individual is placed in this context. The final question addressed in this chapter concerns the becoming of educational psychologists and their profession. Starting from the self, the argument then shifts onto the practice of educational psychology using some ideas from MacIntyre (2000).

1. DILEMMAS

Dilemma, quandary, predicament, problem...these are words which I find myself using quite frequently, at least since I entered the profession of educational psychologist. Nothing seems to be straightforward and I often find myself in situations in which some serious decisions with far reaching consequences need to be taken fast. Mulling over the alternative choices has to stop at a certain point and the defining action needs to be taken. Besides this, I frequently find myself questioning my attitudes and my stance towards people in general and those I meet in my work in particular. I am not comfortable being in this position and my discomfort makes me feel as though I ought not to be the person fulfilling this role. However, part of this study deals with the realisation that the fact that I do feel discomfort might make me the kind of person who ought to have this role. If I were to be comfortable fulfilling this role and taking decisions, then that may be the time to worry. The emotions accompanying dilemmas may be an indication of the importance of the issue for the individual (Skoe, *et al.*, 2002). Since the time I commenced graduate studies, I was encouraged to write about what concerns me, and this served to increase my awareness of these issues. Writing has highlighted these concerns and given them a different form. "Writing down my experiences … seemed to be a creative act which continually lit up new possibilities in what I had seen" (Field, 1990, p. 44).

The ideas written throughout this time and the accompanying exclamation marks indicated that I was passionate about quite a few points and I realised that I was starting to be faced with compromises which I was not willing to make. The realisation that what I was writing about concerned the ethics of working did not occur until later – it was in fact my supervisor who pointed it out to me and my first reaction was to grimace. For me, morality and psychology meant Kohlberg (1979), whose moral developmental process I had studied for my undergraduate examinations. It did not seem to resonate with what I was thinking about and, more so, feeling intensely about. There was no mention there of the essential role which feelings have in a person's moral orientation when resolving a conflict (Skoe, *et al.*, 2002). Gilligan (1993) did criticise Kohlberg's definition of principled reasoning as too objective and narrowly rational and was named *Woman of the Year* following the immediate impact which her views had.

In my undergraduate degree, I went through the motions of the ethics modules prescribed, but tended to find the topic rather boring. It seemed to me to be stating the obvious, as I also had the impression that the ethics of practice were unproblematic and cut and dried, with easily defined right and wrong. I took it for granted that, when one was a professional, there were things which one did and others which one did not do, for ethical reasons. The examples which were brought up to highlight ethical issues seemed to me to be almost banal and I recall feeling quite exasperated at times, thinking that our lecturers must have a very poor notion of us, if they felt we did not know about issues like confidentiality, professional-client boundaries etc. I held most of my lecturers in great esteem and decided that they had to 'do' the ethics topic because it had to be done anyway. So to me, ethics was a topic which had to be suffered.

I had a similar attitude towards ethical codes of practice. If a psychologist needed an ethical code to tell him/her that sexual conduct with clients was wrong, what was that person doing as a psychologist? According to Francis (2002), out of the different roles that ethical codes have, the legalistic role is not their primary purpose. He maintains that the function of codes of ethics is to set and maintain aspirational standards of human value. Ethical codes of professional practice do not seem to provide answers to situations which are more mundane, more recurrent in everyday practice, but which nonetheless have far-reaching consequences. "No code can … solve all of the ethical issues of a profession…. Professional ethics codes cannot… act as a conscience for the individuals who are engaged in research, teaching, and clinical practice" (Kitchener, 1996, p. 369). I seldom gave codes of practice their due importance – I took them for granted. I am not here writing about the possibility of practitioners violating the basic codes mentioned above as this is not the area in which my focus lies. As Small (2001) delineates, "we should not confuse a code of ethics with rules designed to guard against deliberate misconduct" (p. 389).

He cites Burgess (1989, p. 61) to emphasise this point: "When only outstanding and outrageous cases are defined as matters for ethical concern, then the daily perplexities, interactions and decisions occurring in the field may well be perceived as merely 'personal'. Ethics then becomes an academic subject, consisting primarily of abstract concepts counterposed by shocking violations" (Small, 2001, p. 404).

Although Small is writing about ethics in research, I want to make the same distinction in practice. The area which interests me concerns "the actions of people acting with good intentions, who at worst can be charged with haste or insensitivity" (ibid., p. 389). What I want to write about are those everyday issues where black and white do not exist but where one is faced with various in-betweens. I hesitate to mention the colour grey because an in-between need not necessarily consist of some black and some white. This would be suggestive of the danger of being insular and of missing out on new, unanticipated possibilities which Soja (1998) warns against in dialectic reasoning. "Two terms are never enough, [Lefebvre] would repeatedly write. *Il y a toujours l'Autre.* There is always the Other, a third term that disrupts, disorders, and begins to reconstitute the conventional binary opposition into an-Other that comprehends but is more than just the sum of two parts" (p. 31).

These in-between situations are so much a part and parcel of what makes our lives that they are almost non-situations in that there may not appear to be decision points to mark them. They may be smaller issues which "are part of our daily practice [so that] it is all too easy to forget that we are actually making ethical decisions at all" (Carrington et al., 2002, p. 30). They are consistent and constant dilemmas. We put them off and try to ignore them sometimes but are constantly faced by them. It may be that we do not even call them dilemmas, although I think that the word still describes what I am writing about here. Billig et al. (1988) use the term 'contrary themes' without which individuals cannot experience dilemmas. These authors stress the dilemmatic nature of ideology which comprises contrary themes.

> Our concern is…with the dilemmatic preconditions, in other words with those contrary themes which under normal circumstances are reflected in people's thoughts. In fact, the existence of the contrary themes ensures that there is a need for thought.… The contrary themes enable people to discuss and puzzle over their everyday life, and in this respect the rhetorical skills of argument are closely linked to the skills of thinking (Billig et al., 1988, p. 3).

This resonates with one of the major themes of this book; on the acknowledgement of uncertainty as prevalent in research and practice and with the idea of the person as non-unitary (Hollway, 1994). Billig et al. (1988) in fact refer to their approach of social psychology as rhetorical, thus moving away from Festinger's (1957 in ibid.) influential theory of cognitive dissonance. The rhetorical approach maintains that

> common sense contains conflicting, indeed dissonant, themes. [It] provides the individual with the seeds for contrary themes, which can conflict dramatically in dilemmatic situations. Because these are seeds, not flowers, all is not fully systematised. Contained within the conflicting general principles are many different possibilities, which may on occasions give rise to argument and debate. Rather than apply their systems unthinkingly, people must also deliberate and

> argue about which seeds need planting at which times in order to develop into flowers. And when people so deliberate or argue, their thinking has a dilemmatic quality (p. 20).

Standish (2001) calls the view of ethics which I put forward "that broader conception in which it is recognised that values permeate our lives" (p. 487) and says that it is different from "the ways in which the ethical has been reconceived in the modern world. The ethical comes in, as it were, at points of conflict – where there is a question over confidentiality, where there are competing interests, where a research finding is sensitive in some way....The ethical is confined to what is sometimes (equally restrictively) called 'social morality'" (p. 487). Standish (2002c) also makes this point in his editorial when he writes about "the ways in which our attraction towards stereotypes in ethical reasoning, for example, or our inclination to think of ethics in terms of moral dilemmas, can cause us to lose sight of the textures of our language, the fabric of community, the daily patterns of our action and interaction, upon which moral life so much depends."

These issues are addressed by the ethical codes of professional bodies and perpetuated by research and consequent articles on the difficulties faced by professionals when ethical dilemmas arise. In fact, the Code of Ethics and Conduct (2006) issued by the British Psychological Society points out that "despite every care being taken, ethical difficulties will occur" (p. 7). Standish (2002c) maintains that one ought to be aware of the values with which one lives, and works, and know that such values are in constant formation and construction. I apply to practice what Pring (2001) argues with reference to research: Is it "sufficient to think in terms of principles, codes and rules [?] It may be more important, from an ethical point of view, to consider much more carefully the virtues of the researcher than the principles he or she espouses" (p. 407). Ethics are not handy only when such predicaments arise – they permeate our constant living. Carrington et al. (2002) write that in many cases, educational psychologists take decisions without even being aware that there is an underlying ethical issue present. Standish (2002c) also makes this point in his editorial when he says that "all philosophy of education, all research in education, is inevitably about ethics in some degree". As one can note, he first says that ethics is in all philosophy of education and then in all education. Billig et al. (1988) in fact emphasise that in everyday discourse one can note the reproduction of the "great problems of philosophy" (p. 6) which reproduction takes the form of dilemmas.

> Even when solutions are found by individuals – at least solutions for the everyday reproduction of the underlying dilemma – other problems emerge as the ideologically constituted dilemma expresses itself in other forms. In this way, the ideology is not reproduced as a closed system for talking about the world. Instead it is reproduced as an incomplete set of contrary themes, which continually give rise to discussion, argumentation and dilemmas (Billig et al., 1988, p. 6).

There is a relationship between ethics and ethical codes of practice which is interesting and paradoxical. The decision points are there and we are the ones who ultimately have to take the responsibility of deciding. This is one objection which

Small (2001) makes towards codes of ethics, saying that "they are misnamed, since ethics is by its nature bound up with individual decision, and so cannot be legislated." (p. 389) Thus, although we may feel protected by our ethical code of practice, we cannot escape the terrifying reality that ultimately, we are ethical not because we follow the code of practice, but because we reinvent, rejustify and reaffirm them (or otherwise) with every decision that we take. I am drawing here on Derrida's paradoxical decision-making moment in his differentiation between justice and law. Although "only a decision is just" (Derrida, 1992, p. 24), still, the act of applying a rule involves the legal, and it may not necessarily be just. For a law to be just, there must be 'fresh judgement' in that the judgement cannot be passed *only* in conformity to a law. "In short, for a decision to be just and responsible, it must, in its proper moment if there is one, be both regulated and without regulation: it must conserve the law and also destroy it or suspend it enough to have to reinvent it in each case, rejustify it, at least reinvent it in the reaffirmation and the new and free confirmation of its principle. Each case is other, each decision is different and requires an absolutely unique interpretation, which no existing, coded rule can or ought to guarantee absolutely" (ibid., p. 23). I begin to understand why Kierkegaard calls the decision a madness and will refer to this again later on.

2. DILEMMAS IN PRACTICE

Birdsall and Hubert (2000, in Smith and Smith, 2001) attempt to define that true ethical dilemmas "are just that – dilemmas. In their complexity, they share the following characteristics:

- There are reasonable choices between two or more courses of action.
- Each choice presents significant potential consequences.
- Each course of action can be supported by ethical principles.
- The selection of either course will compromise an ethical principle." (p. 440)

The last point is the one which identifies the reasons for which I experience the aforementioned discomfort. The dilemma consists of the fact that whichever decision one takes, means that one has decided not only in favour of one course of action, but also against another. Thus, one has made a decision about which ethical principle to sacrifice. The above definition has a greater resemblance to the original use of the term dilemma, a classic example of which is Sartre's (in Kaufman, 1989) story of a pupil who sought his advice. This young man lived with his mother and was her one consolation in a life of deep affliction. He wanted to join the Free French Forces, also to avenge his brother's death in the German offensive of 1940. Knowing that his mother lived solely for him, he realised that by staying with his mother he would be concretely helping her to live, whereas there were no guarantees that his actions in the Forces would serve any concrete purpose as he might be given administrative work rather than fighting.

> Consequently, he found himself confronted by two very different modes of action; the one concrete, immediate, but directed towards only one individual; and the other an action addressed to an end infinitely greater, a national collectivity, but for that very reason ambiguous – and it might be frustrated

> on the way. At the same time, he was hesitating between two kinds of morality; on the one side the morality of sympathy, of personal devotion and, on the other side, a morality of wider scope but of more debatable validity. He had to choose between those two (Sartre in Kaufman, 1989 – internet source).

I do not want to confine the use of this term to this narrower kind of decision-making. My view of dilemmas tallies with Billig et al.'s (1998) whose concern is "to show how ordinary life ... is shaped by dilemmatic qualities" (p. 9) and readers should be aware that future references to dilemmas have this definition. I earlier referred to such situations as nondecisions, especially as one can get used to the discomfort mentioned above and it therefore stops being uncomfortable. Perhaps this is a survival tactic, that one looks towards the stance, or position, or state of being where the least discomfort is experienced.

When discussing their mental health outreach system, Rowe et al. (2001) conclude that it is not possible to do away with the ambiguity with which their jobs are laden and a constant decision is faced to infringe on or to respect the clients' right to choose whether treatment is wanted or not. "...this entails living on the cusp of a dilemma, erring at the last moment on the side of clients' safety from harm and death but pushing the envelope of clinical comfort in acknowledgement of their autonomy and proven ability to survive on the street" (p. 406). A number of experiences in fact recount that the individual circumstances of dilemmas lead practitioners to take decisions 'situationally' as the specific contexts within which the dilemmas occur are 'inextricably bound' and influence future action (Goodwin et al., 2003, p. 568). Even after decisions are taken, practitioners are left "feeling uncertain about decisions, responsible for outcomes, self-doubting of their professional capabilities and reluctant to face the next challenge" (McAuliffe and Sudbery, 2005, p. 23). This is because the decision taken, as well as the route not chosen, both continue to haunt the person deciding. It also reflects the previously mentioned attitudes and values which the person has (Standish, 2001, 2002c).

However, I imagine that this 'haunting' is only true of those practitioners who feel themselves faced with such a decision. According to a survey by Lindsay and Colley (1995), 37% of psychologists contacted reported that they did not face ethical dilemmas in their work – the ensuing question being whether this is a true reflection of their absence or a lack of awareness of the complexities in their daily practice. Surely there is no question of such practitioners being 'haunted' either by the decision taken, or by the non-decision. One wonders whether they would agree with Gersch's belief that "the current zeitgeist is prone to significant change, uncertainty and anxiety, and [that] these factors need to inform future ... psychology practice" (2004, p. 142). On a personal note, when I have shared these thoughts with other practitioners, I was sometimes told that these were issues which can be solved in supervision, or in therapy, and also that my thoughts reflected my lack of experience in the field. Although my first reaction to such well-intentioned comments was to feel inadequate and insecure, I then realised that I would rather not have these issues 'solved', if this meant that I would not be as aware of the minutiae of such complexities.

It is as though it is thought that, through experience, one learns how to cope better and how to become more efficient and effective in one's practice. I think this encourages practitioners to 'get on with it', thus leaving the ethics for the moment of decision and blinding them to the factors which contribute to this moment. Derrida calls this the necessity of the impossible decision, which is so because of the ordeal which one goes through before the decision is taken. If one is to make a free decision, then one cannot follow a prescripted path of decision-making – that "would only be the programmable application or unfolding of a calculable process" (Derrida, 1992, p. 24). The moment of uncertainty and suspense of the undecidable is necessary if the practitioner is to make a real decision. And "the undecidable remains caught, lodged, at least as a ghost – but an essential ghost – in every decision" (Derrida, 1992, p. 24). This is the reason for which practitioners may prefer to do away with decisions, and to prefer to have policies and procedures to follow. When one has to follow a policy, this keeps the matter in the realm of the public, of the practice, and it does not have its impact on the private and personal. The decision has been taken for the practitioner and is made explicit in the policy document. Some practitioners even carry the document around with them to prove that such and such a way is the only way forward. Small (2001) cites Roger Homan to push forward his point of the possible harmful effects of codes of ethics: "By defining moral obligations in a formal fashion, they give the impression that these may be satisfied by a single procedure of compliance, rather than through a *continuing* process of considering the ethical aspects of one's actions" (p. 391, my own emphasis). When decisions are taken, in the Derridian sense, the ensuing emotions are as McAuliffe and Sudbury (2005) mentioned before.

Another factor which contributes to the aforementioned madness in making a decision is the urgency with which decisions need to be taken. As I mentioned in the beginning of this chapter, decisions often need to be taken fast. There is no time to gather all the information which the practitioner may feel is necessary, and it may be that the practitioner never feels ready to take the decision – but it needs to be done, and immediately.

> ...a just decision is always required *immediately*, 'right away'. It cannot furnish itself with the infinite information and the unlimited knowledge of conditions, rules or hypothetical imperative that could justify it. And even if it did have all that at its disposal, even if it did give itself the time, all the time and the necessary facts about the matter, the moment of *decision, as such*, always remains a finite moment of urgency and precipitation, since it must not be the consequence or the effect of this theoretical or historical knowledge, of this reflection or this deliberation, since it always marks the interruption of the juridico- or ethico- or politico-cognitive deliberation that precedes it, that *must* precede it. The instant of decision is a madness, says Kierkegaard (Derrida, 1992, p. 26).

In Chapters 5 and 9, I explore the ordeal which I experienced prior to taking a decision concerning a child and refer to the above arguments again.

Perhaps this is what Paul Standish is referring to when he says that ethics ought not to come in only at points of conflict, which I am referring to as dilemmas. As Billig et al. (1988) claim, this dilemmatic approach brings forward a different image of the thinker from the individual with inner unity. Later in this chapter I refer to psychoanalytic theory which sees the ego of the individual as constantly moving in and out of stability (Klein, 1997) in what I call a process of becoming. Dilemmas are ever-present and enmeshed in our work. I believe that part of becoming a helping professional in general, and in my case an educational psychologist, is the acceptance and, indeed, embracing of uncertainty and dilemmas in our work. It is a question of living with dilemmas.

3. THE 'RUNAWAY' WORLD WHICH REQUIRES ORDER AND PRECISION

However, there are professionals who do not share this feeling. Could it be that the psychologists in Lindsay and Colley's survey (1995) have different ideas of what ethics and dilemmas are and different ways of dealing with them because of the variety in training given and received? In the same way that I had a different perspective of ethics in my undergraduate course, there must be a number of different points of view. Do different schools of education and care encourage different styles of ethical practice? I believe that this could be possible in various ways. The persons actually carrying out the training could have such beliefs themselves and also the trainees chosen to enter the course could have such tendencies.

At one point during my training, I recall being shown by other trainees from other training courses a problem-solving approach which they had been taught and that could be applied to situations faced. It seemed to me to be a step by step system which ensured that all the factors in a problematic situation were taken into account. Since I am a person who is sometimes plagued by insecurity, my instant reaction was that I ought to learn one of these approaches. That way, I could become a good practitioner and manage to solve many problems. I would learn where each bit of the problem went in the scheme of the approach and it would prompt me to think through to the possibilities which could help the family and child involved.

These approaches and strategies are very helpful in that they attempt to ensure that all the possible options and outcomes are considered. Several papers are written mentioning their use (e.g. Webster and Bond, 2002; Carrington, Griffin, Hollis and Parry, 2002; Franey, 2002). However, is it possible that the eagerness in me to work with systems might stem from a wish to put things in their proper place, to decrease mess and untidiness, in the hope that when the confusion is sorted, the solution emerges? "The surrogate of the formal system entices us away from the stubborn messiness of everyday life in an ideal extension of the epistemology of 'what works'" (Standish, 2001, p. 503). I realise that unease with the complexity which abounds in my work spurs the attraction towards such systems. It also looks and sounds very modern and 'professional'. It impresses people, this manner of manipulating situations round, turning chaos into solutions, just like it struck me. Standish (2005a) calls this a form of "closed economy" and says that there "is something curiously self-reinforcing, self-perpetuating and, for some, seductive about this entire way of thinking" (p. 57). It is possible that we become lulled into a sweet sense of security. This point will be taken up further in the next section when Hollway's (1994) suggestion of non-unitary subjectivity is outlined.

ACKNOWLEDGING THE COMPLEX SELF

Besides the complexity in society and in the practitioner's work with people (which I will expand on later), besides the complexity of people's lives and the difficulties unravelling the problems which surround families and their children, there is another kind of complexity, which may be forgotten owing to our outward-looking attitude. I refer to the complexity which comprises the researcher and practitioner. The latter is no less a person, just like the children and families with whom she is involved, and is also made up of contradictions and complexities which interact with those that other people have, and also those in the workplace. The educational psychologist is expected to present as an expert in the field, someone decisive and in authority, who will be able to find the solution beyond the mess and inconsistencies. Self-doubt would very much be discordant with this image. This belief in a person who is confident and secure is contagious and as practitioners we can feel that this is the way we are, or, if not, that this is the way we ought to be. Webster and Bond (2002) write about structuring uncertainty in a special issue of the Educational and Child Psychology on Ethics in Practice: "Accepting that professionals operate in complex, uncertain and unpredictable circumstances, how can we find ways of reducing the unknown?" (p. 17). They suggest systematic procedures to enable options to be considered when a decision is to be reached.

However, I suggest that it might be interesting to attempt to befriend the contradictory state of being and to view it as part and parcel of who we are. Klein (1997) writes about splitting in the psyche, which means that the nature of the latter is full of contradictions. Through splitting, the psyche separates the good from the bad in an attempt to cope with an internal struggle or conflict. When splitting as a dynamic works successfully, the effect is that the person has inner unity and she feels that for the moment, she knows what to do or think. However, when it comes to issues that matter, the process of splitting is not simple. Thus a person may not be able to decide one course of action as she feels pulled towards more than one possibility. This may be difficult to cope with as we are not accustomed to variability and contradiction in our definition of ourselves. It overturns "the western view that the distinguishing mark of humanity is reason and rationality" (Frosh, 1987, p. 25, in Hollway, 1994, p. 29).

Hollway (1994) argues that "people's accounts are always contingent: upon available time and discourses (the regimes of truth which govern the directions in which one's thinking can go); upon the relationships within which the accounts are produced and upon the context of events recounted; upon power and the defences in operation against formulating different versions because of their self-threatening implications" (p. 39). A person who can find a unitary answer and reason for events and happenings is one, according to Hollway (1994), who might possibly be ignoring others. She developed a theory of multiple and contradictory subjectivity through her critique of the unitary individual subject, so that the suppression of inconsistency and variability may be stopped. What is the effect if one applies this to the practitioner mentioned above who is turned to for expert advice on important matters involving children in schools and their families?

We are all conditioned by the discourse of the rational unitary subject prescribing norms and subjectivity. Thus we feel that we ought to be "consistent with the (internally consistent) values that one rationally upholds" (Hollway, 1994, p. 69). So which part is to be suppressed? This is 'prescribed' by rationality and anxiety – the part that contradicts the conscious intentional positioning. Hollway refers to Klein's relational defences against anxiety to explain how the inherent split in the psyche needs to move towards integrity. It is very difficult to produce an account which acknowledges contradictions, and describes the detail and diversity of events and analyses experience in terms which go beyond the unitary, rational subject. Defences are maintained to achieve integrity with an energy which is equivalent to the energy of the original repressed desire.

Hollway (1994) maintains that the continuous attempt to manage anxiety, to protect oneself, is never finally accomplished. Anxiety provides a continuous, driven motive for the negotiation of power in relations. The multiple and contradictory forces have their effects on power relations, on subjectivities, on positions in discourses and practices and therefore on the reproduction of certain knowledges and not others. Hollway's concept of subjectivity is dynamic, non-unitary, extra-rational and is discoverable only within inter-subjective relations. Hollway and Jefferson (2001) then write about defended persons who "invest in discourses when these offer positions which provide protection against anxiety and therefore support to identity" (p. 24). The practitioner may feel the need of this kind of protection. As will be expanded further in the next chapter, each challenge led me to question my competence and I yearned for the confidence and security which I perceived in other professionals. Uncertainty seemed not to be an issue for them and neither was self-doubt. Moreover, situations in schools served to enhance this image, as I was appealed to for solutions to difficulties which were experienced with children. However, through Klein (1997), Hollway (1994) and, as will be seen later, with Bion (1994), a different possibility of the practitioner can be seen, especially one who works with children. This practitioner can acknowledge the differences and inconsistencies in dilemmas, in her own accounts and also in those of others without needing to suppress them or dismiss them as distortions. Rather than endangering the confidence which others put on such a practitioner, this stance is actually a better guarantee that a child will not be needlessly categorised in an unthinking attempt to rationalise and put messy situations in order. Such a practitioner is engaged in a process of becoming, possibly without the knowledge of which destination, rather than perceiving herself as having become an expert.

COMPLEXITY IN A RUNAWAY WORLD

Standish's idea (2001) that we are ruled by 'what works' is a reflection of the manner in which society deals with its difficulties, in that they are categorised and classified into the appropriate slots. This is the way in which the capitalist world in general is being currently run, with its ever faster pace and its emphasis on solution-oriented effectiveness. Nixon cites Beck and Beck-Gernsheim (2002) when he uses their metaphor of 'a runaway world', which is "characterised by a rapid acceleration in the pace of individualisation" (Nixon, 2003, p. 4). Incompatibility and restlessness typify this runaway world, which is rated differently by various groups in society, depending on what they stand to gain from it. While some deprecate what they see as "the breakdown of relationships and connectivity, the erosion of civic purposefulness and engagement, and the loss of boundary and identity" (p. 4), others focus on the increase in inequalities which emerges from such a world, and others still like the new freedoms in this "world of infinite possibility within which any notion of 'limit' is rendered off-limits" (p. 4).

These conditions have made life very much more complex. If one merely notes the increase in choices which people have, one can realise that there is more material which one has to decide about, and to decide fast, otherwise the decision will be taken for one by some other entity. Nixon (2003) mentions the restless and migrant travelling life for academics "both literally and metaphorically, a nomadic life, a life spent in cars, aeroplanes and trains, on the telephone or the internet, supported by the mass media, a transnational life stretching across frontiers" (p. 4). On a similar note, Buchanan (2005) writes about how contemporary life "is truly marvellous in the old-fashioned sense of the term, something literally to be marvelled at" (p. 26). It is possible to be still half asleep in Paris, drinking Brazilian coffee, thinking about a lecture one is going to give in Sicily during the day, "while in the background, his bedside radio conveys in blank tones the news of the day – catastrophes in the Orient, the Tour de France leader-board, a recent Gallup poll, and so forth" (in Buchanan, 2005, p. 26).

Nixon's specific concern, in noting the changes within society, is how this all affects the academic profession and he writes about how universities and academic work have had to adapt (Nixon, 2001a, 2001c, 2003, 2004b; Nixon and Walker, 2004c; Nixon et al., 1997). Although this writing is not focussed on the same institution, much of what he says seems applicable to the helping professions and the institutions which house these professions. The helping professions could be said to be "becoming 'an increasingly part-time profession', 'an increasingly managed profession', and 'an increasingly capitalistic profession…'" (Rhoades and Slaughter, 1998, p. 34–35 in Nixon, 2001c, p. 232), with all the ramifications that such conditions bring. The work of helping professionals is adapted to the changing division of labour in the market. "The combined influences of the state, institutional managers and the market" (Miller, 1995, p. 56 in Nixon, 2001c, p. 233) are determining what we do and consequently the manner in which we do it.

> We ought not to be sanctimonious about this. We have all, as intellectual workers, in varying degrees had to learn to be bi-lingual: to utter the standard platitudes of managerialism, while adopting within our own street culture of academic journals and collegial dialogue an older demotic. We cannot afford to ignore the language of managerialism, but nor can we afford to ignore its deep ideological drift. The language of inputs and outputs, of clients and products, of delivery and measurement, of providers and users, is not just a different way of talking about the same thing. It radically alters what we are talking about. It constitutes a new way of thinking about teaching and learning. Ultimately, it affects how we teach and how we learn. It has designs upon us and upon what we understand by educational studies (Nixon, 2004b, p. 246).

This is, I fear, what is happening to practitioners in the caring professions also, and has been influencing the manner in which we interact with families and children. There is an ever-growing insistence on accountability, on targets, on levels of attainment etc. which apparently starts out with the purposes of having the public have more control over where their tax-payments are going. However, "underlying this ostensible aim of accountability *to the public* the real requirements are for accountability *to regulators, to departments of government, to funders, to legal standards.* The new forms of accountability impose forms of central control – quite often indeed *a range of different and mutually inconsistent* forms of central control." (O'Neill, 2002, p. 52–53 italics in original, in Nixon, 2004b, p. 247). Thus, as expanded further in Chapters 10 and 11, rather than helping to reinstate public trust in the services which ought to help the public, this mode of management brings about what O'Neill calls a 'culture of suspicion' which is used to justify the centralised control of these public institutions.

Nixon thus calls for a re-definition of professionalism (in his case of academics) in terms of underlying commitments and purposes with reference to consideration of others. The quality-control mechanisms and accountability procedures must not make this emergent professionalism submissive to their demands. In fact, "when push comes to shove" (2001c, p. 231), the allegiance of practitioners is owed to the values which are implicit in practice, "in the interests of their own professionalism" (ibid.). These are the intrinsic goods which MacIntyre (2000) mentions and which I will write about further in Chapter 11. Their main characteristic is that "their achievement is a good for the whole community who participate in the practice" (p. 190) whereas external goods are what institutions are mostly concerned with as these "are structured in terms of power and status, and they distribute money, power and status as rewards" (ibid., p. 194).

Nixon et al. (1997) do not ask from us a cynicism which leads us to leave the institutions in which we practise and to retreat from the contaminated world. With MacIntyre, they claim that practice cannot be sustained without the institution and thus call for a "critical distance" (p. 13) between the practitioner and the institutional context to place a limit on the vulnerability of the practitioner "to the acquisitiveness and competitiveness of the institution" (ibid.). It would thus become part of the practitioner's "*professional* duty to adopt an explicitly oppositional stance to policies that prioritise external goods of the institution or militate against the internal goods … for example, policies that are aimed at increasing competition, generating acquisitiveness or reproducing inequality" (Nixon et al., 1997, p. 13).

In this book, there is a call to return to the use of words which represent fundamental concepts that have been in never-ending discussion and debate, at least since the beginning of philosophy as we know it. Words like good, flourishing, justice and morality are used intentionally, as I believe that we do not meet them much in present day readings. Policies and plans, particularly in the field of education and psychology, are constantly being issued, and have very ambitious names (such as *For all children to succeed: A new network organisation for quality education in Malta*, 2005). However, it seems that we do not engage with the concepts behind such words. We seem to use the words because they sound good, and are also catchy and bold. But the discussion of justice is missing in these documents – it is obviously implied, but it is not put on the agenda and explored. It is as though we have decided that such concepts are oldspeak, that these issues, ideas and thoughts have been dealt with and we all know what to do with them. We leave it up to a philosopher of education to engage with these concepts and then say that s/he is removed from the everyday life of education. We replace such vocabulary with another, which is more easily handled and which is more influenced by capitalism and performativity.

However, the nature of such fundamental concepts is that they are always evolving and growing – they are always in the process of becoming, and so are we when we engage with them. The vocabulary predominant in today's documents is reachable, can be operationalised and perhaps even quantified. But it is too prescribed, too much is taken for granted. We bandy today's words around so that we have become desensitised to their meaning and implications. Documents consider inclusive education and selection (streaming and special education) in the same breath, without unpacking or analysis (Inclusive and Special Education Review, 2005). We need to return to the concepts of good, justice, eudaimonia etc. to start investigating our actions, our motivations and our results. Standish (2004) says that the cause of such situations is "the colonisation of thought by performativity" (p. 497). He calls for the "dismantling [of] the oppressive and totalizing structures that have come to dominate educational practice.... On the face of it, 'oppressive' and 'totalizing' appear more or less conventional political terms. What is at issue here is much more a matter of the colonising of thought by performativity. The consequences of this colonisation are that we are progressively disabled from thinking in certain ways, ways that are vital to education, as they are to the pursuit of truth itself" (Standish, 2004, p. 497).

4. WHAT KIND OF PSYCHOLOGIST AM I BECOMING?

Whereas I cannot say with certainty what kind of psychologist I am becoming, and am using this opportunity to explore it further, I remember with a smile which is half amused and half nostalgic what I used to believe being a psychologist was. Although I never bought into the joke that a psychologist can read someone else's 'mind', I did believe that I would know more than everybody else the reasons for this, that and the other. I believed that others would defer to my opinion and, while not revelling in this belief in terms of power, I did subscribe to the thought that I would be the one others would come to. I thought I would be in a better position to help others. I would be one of the experts whom people call upon to solve their difficulties.

How is it that I now find myself shrinking from a telephone when I am told that a call has come through for me? Where is the knowledge which I believed I would have? I do not feel as I believed an expert should feel when working with people. I feel confused, frightened, worried and am sometimes even close to panic. A feeling of inadequacy, which is difficult to cope with, threatens to overcome me and I find myself fighting both the demons without, as well as those within me. For not only do I expect the expert from myself, but I am also expected to be the expert by the persons that I work with, be they parents, teachers or other professionals.

Schön (2000) has shown that a crisis of confidence has come about in professional knowledge even among the professionals themselves. The very practices which were supposed to alleviate the difficulties in society were further perpetrating these difficulties and professionals suddenly found themselves in the role of the villain. Knowledge is no longer monopolised by professionals. "The traditional model of professionalism … has sustained a serious sociological attack upon its service ethic and an equally serious epistemological attack upon its assumption of specialist knowledge and expertise" (Nixon et al., 1997, p. 12).

There seems to be a growing awareness of instability, contingency and temporality in every process. Whereas the centre and basis of everything was seen as the individual, now the post-structuralist idea is that the individual is also regarded as something which changes and fluctuates. Rather than having "the knowing self as the foundation of a unified and ordered life" (Nixon *et al.*, 1997, p. 12), the identity of the agent is marked by change and fluctuation. As mentioned earlier, according to Klein (1997), this is the result of the ongoing struggle within the individual as she moves towards integrity. Bauman says that "...the self-organisation of the agents in terms of *life-project* (a concept that assumes a long-term stability; a lasting identity of the habitat, in its duration transcending, or at least commensurate with, the longevity of human life) is displaced by the *process of self-constitution*" (1992, p. 193–194 in Nixon et al., 1997, p. 13).

This is what was most striking in my first reading of MacIntyre (2000), him asking the question *what sort of person am I to become?* (p. 118). The search for *becoming* resonated with questions about the need for constant self-formation. In fact, I changed his question because I believe that I am in a state of becoming already, not only that I will become some day. This has already been touched upon through the mention of Klein's theory of splitting as the psyche moves towards growth, but will be explained further below. This change in perspective from stability to constant fluctuation, however, may require a different kind of professionalism. Rather than being the expert, the professional may be seen as one who has learnt to live with not knowing, with the lack of stability, uncertainty and unpredictability which this brings about. Nixon *et al.* (1997) try to define this new learning profession which is characterised by the "'professionality' which focuses on the quality of practice in contexts that require radically altered relations of power and control" (p. 12).

What, however, makes quality in practice? How does it contribute to our becoming? In considering the internal goods of practice, MacIntyre defines that which motivates our actions in practice, the *telos* of an activity. It is impossible to try and do full justice to MacIntyre's writing here. However, some salient points from MacIntyre's work will be mentioned as it is of great relevance to the points that I am making. This does not mean that I adopt MacIntyre's perspective, but his ideas help me to define more clearly my own position. As Nixon writes (2004c), MacIntyre's book *After Virtue*, which caused great uproar and reactions when it came out, is a dense and complex book and requires multiple readings and possibly also the reading of other authors writing about him in order to start appreciating his suggestions. I have mentioned already what I believe to be the inadequacy of the application model of ethics in practice. Jordan and Meara (1990) write about the significance of the difference between what they call *principle ethics* and *virtue ethics*, and the implications that each has for the professional development and practice of psychologists. While the former emphasise the use of "rational, objective, universal, and impartial principles in the ethical analysis of dilemmas" and focus on acts and choices, virtue ethics "focus on the historically formed character of identifiable persons, [which] character development provides the basis for professional judgement" (p. 107). In other words, one aims to answer the question 'what am I to do?' while the other the question 'who am I to be?'

MacIntyre's work considers the latter and explores the ins and outs of how it works. His definition of practice is problematic when it comes to the helping professions, as it was found to be for the teaching profession (MacIntyre and Dunne, 2002; Dunne, 2003). This is tackled further in Chapter 11. Suffice it to say at present that while MacIntyre claimed that "teaching itself is not a practice" (MacIntyre and Dunne, 2002, p. 5), I follow Dunne's (2003) and Smith's (2003) arguments and argue that the helping professions and teaching are practices and apply some of MacIntyre's ideas on practice to my profession. The practitioner acts out the good not because she is told to do so by any policy or procedure but because this good is valued for its own sake and because it is also good in that it contributes to the flourishing of that practitioner. These are the internal goods of a practice and ought to be distinguished from what he terms as the external goods (which are the concern of institutions), and which "are involved in acquiring money and other material goods; they are structured in terms of power and status, and they distribute money, power and status as rewards" (MacIntyre, 2000, p. 194). Virtues are what help us in our attempt to reach these internal goods but at the same time, as they also contribute to our flourishing, they are also goods in themselves.

> Like any Aristotelian, MacIntyre understands the virtues as acquired excellences of persons, as dispositions to act for the good. On one level, then, virtues are instrumental to goods. At the same time, since the virtues are partly constitutive of our well-being they themselves constitute goods (Higgins, 2003, p. 281).

According to Higgins (2003), MacIntyre mentions three different domains in which we strive for the good. We encounter goods in practices in that as we pursue our practice, we learn about the good as such. The acquisition of virtues enables us to achieve internal goods. "The achievement of those 'goods' requires particular qualities, or dispositions, which are in turn enhanced through that achievement. *I become virtuous through the practice of virtue*" (Nixon, 2004c, p. 118). According to MacIntyre, at the level of practices, virtues are what would help the practitioner to practise with integrity "in the face of institutional expediency" (Higgins, p. 281). This refers to what was mentioned in the previous section about the difficulties of living (and working) in a world with its ever-increasing emphasis on effectiveness, efficiency, accountability etc. Morstyn , for example, writes about the pity that this 'institutional expediency' is managing to do away with sincerity in the therapeutic relationship: "It is quite remarkable how the current obsession with measurement in Evidence-Based Medicine has managed to eliminate something so centrally important as therapist sincerity from general consideration. Therapists who 'fake' sincerity may be very successful in adapting to current cultural conditions but they are ultimately 'just playing the game'" (Morstyn, 2002, p. 328).

The second domain where goods and virtues receive their meaning and substance is in the individual life narrative. We experience different virtues in our own way, according to our individual life – hence the question 'what is *my* good?' The intentions and purposes of our actions can only be seen in light of the context in which those actions take place. "The intentionality and purposefulness of the agent provide human life with its unity and ensures that the virtues cohere within that unity" (Nixon, 2004c, p. 118). The variety of internal goods and virtues which the practitioner encounters at the level of practice belong to the individual when she chooses which are to be relevant to her life, and orders and synthesises them. In this way, the flourishing which a practitioner achieves through practice affects other aspects of that practitioner's life. Thus, not only would goods be worthwhile for their own sake, but they would be relevant for the rest of the practitioner's life, even when she is not practising.

Tradition is important in MacIntyre's third domain, where the virtues are understood as those "qualities the exercise of which leads to the human *telos*" (MacIntyre, 1984a, p. 184 in Higgins, 2003, p. 282). In the same way that individuals prioritise the virtues differently according to their life, in different traditions, there are different ideas of "what is worth striving for in human life" (ibid.). These three domains influence each other in various ways. "There is … always reciprocity in the process of becoming virtuous. The reciprocity refers to my relation to my own practice, my relation to the contexts and situations within which I practise, and my relation to the continuing traditions within which my practice is located. The motor which drives these virtuous reciprocities is my own agency: my own developing sense of purposefulness and intentionality" (Nixon, 2004c, p. 119).

For my purposes, though, these distinctions help me put forward the idea that objective principles simply do not help practitioners enough in the dilemmas of practice – as Standish said, it is not only when we are faced with the fork in the road that we decide to use ethics (2001). We are constantly forming ourselves, constituting ourselves, according to the goods which we have put as important for us to fulfil our potential. Here I do not follow MacIntyre strictly but adapt his ideas: any reader of MacIntyre knows that MacIntyre's work aims to re-establish certainty and that the *telos* is aimed at by going back to the traditions and canonical texts of a particular culture. Smith (2003) outlines MacIntyre's argument that "we live in a world which has largely lost the resources needed properly to think about the ends and goals of life, and to oppose the manipulation of preferences on the part of those with an interest in exploiting us" (p. 313). I have already suggested that the practitioner learns to work with inconsistencies and uncertainties towards a *telos*. When the need to go back to the original point arises, the psychologist can ask "Why did I want to become a psychologist in the first place?" This question serves to remind the practitioner to acknowledge the complexities which are people. Hollway (1994) writes "I wanted to study psychology because I wanted to understand people (that phrase has come to sound trite and naïve, but I think it needs to be reclaimed for serious psychology)" (p. 2). This resembles Blake et al.'s (1998) observation: "Teachers and academics who entered their profession out of a sense that they liked children or young people, or were engrossed in their specialist subject, are confronted with new and alien imperatives" (p. 4). In the case of educational psychology, I suggest that although the original question does not serve to put to rest other questions and doubts (which is what MacIntyre would like) – it aims to put the psychologist back on track where she stops striving towards certainty where this may be premature, and acknowledges the mess and difficulties of working with people.

> "Perhaps even more important is the fact that such reflection relies on the constant rediscovery of these goods in their spark and substance. Ethical ideals that speak to everyone regardless of their location in and across some variety of local practices are likely to be banal" (Higgins, 2003, p. 284).

So in asking the question mentioned above, a constant rediscovery of the goods is possible. This is a very important point and is the reason behind my insistence on the continuous verb 'becoming' instead of 'become' because there will never be an end – the end always recedes.

> ...internal goods cannot be the same as the standards of excellence. This ambiguity is resolved by making a distinction between ideals conceived and excellence achieved (1990, p. 62). The *telos* of a practice, the vision of the fully perfected work receded like the horizon as we approach it; by definition it outstrips our ability to realise it. (Even though the *telos* is revised as the practice evolves, each form of the *telos* serves as a horizon for actions within the practice, just as sailors may choose to set course by a different star without having reached the first star or expecting to reach the second.) But it is in light of that *telos* that we can name the kind and degree of actual achievements made by outstanding if fallible practitioners. Internal goods are not the distant points on the horizon but the journeys toward the good (Higgins, 2003, p. 286).

Moreover, excelling in one's practice is not only to strive to achieve what is termed as excellent, but also to go beyond the existing standards. There is simply no room for the feeling that one has reached a state with which one should be satisfied and contented. The search for more is ever-present in the virtuous practitioner. These points further serve to change the picture of the practitioner from one who knows and who is an expert to one who is more open to not knowing and to uncertainty. The swampy marshlands which Schön (2000) mentions are not to be steered away from but almost states of being to be embraced as opportunities for flourishing. Thus, the importance which MacIntyre attributes to practice is understood when he says that practices are not places where virtuous dispositions can work – they are in themselves 'moral sources' of such dispositions. So practices are not only opportunities for practitioners where they can do good, but also where they encounter the good; a move away from the practitioner who comes in with her tools, fixes something which is wrong, and leaves the problematic situation solved. It is, however, a move towards the practitioner who engages with the situation, understands that the engagement requires her virtues and also that it will provide her with the opportunity to synthesise virtues, and ultimately to contribute to her own flourishing which, by the way, will not cease.

As previously mentioned, the latter practitioner may not fit as well within the institution within which she practises. This is because of the serious threat to the continuity and integrity of institutions, which threat is brought about by the increase in acceleration in the pace of individualisation of the aforementioned 'runaway world'. In a succinct summary of MacIntyre's argument, Smith (2003) describes "our age [as] a fissiparous and fragmented one" (p. 312). Institutions are important and have traditionally given us a sense of 'membership' and 'belongingness' (Nixon, 2003). However, the accelerating individualisation threatens the above and emphasises difference more than commonality. These days, more and more frequently, 'institutional expediency' makes demands on the practitioner and causes her to cut corners, to make do, and to base decisions on what works. However, although the practice is "always vulnerable to the acquisitiveness and competitiveness of the institution" (Nixon, 1997, p. 13), it cannot be sustained without it. "Those values, skills and understandings are conditional … upon professionals recognising their own needs as learners; and that recognition is, in turn, shaped by institutional factors … Insofar as professionalism constitutes a commitment to the internal goods of learning, it provides a critical distance between the practitioner and the institutional contexts within which the practitioner operates. The practitioner lays claims to professionalism by virtue of that critical distance" (Nixon, 1997, p. 13). This is the intimate and crucial relationship between institution and practice.

When calling for a new emergent professionalism, Nixon (2001) thus specifies that shared understanding and open dialogue are necessary qualities and that claims to professionalism ought not to be dependent on status or self-regulation. Values and practices constitute this emergent professionalism which seeks to answer the question 'why I do what I do?' (Nixon, 2001, p. 234). It is this moral purposefulness of practice which ought to be emphasised in the training of new entrants to the profession, more specifically, "the values of care and affection, of critical engagement and dialogue, of public concern and welfare" (p. 237). Although Nixon chooses these virtues as ones which would be desirable in the academic profession, I find that they are equally necessary in the caring professions working with children. This moral purposefulness is "a formative process which requires the ongoing exercise of deliberation" (Nixon, 2004c, p. 120).

> That is what it means to live in 'a runaway world': the experience, certainly, of chronic uncertainty, but the hope, also, of reconciling that uncertainty with a sense of moral purposefulness that necessitates an ongoing search for resolutions that recognise differences of outlook and belief, background and expectation, purpose and condition (Nixon, 2003, p. 10).

CHAPTER 4

UNCERTAINTY IN RESEARCH AND PRACTICE

INTRODUCTION

This chapter is the first of three chapters which rotates around the issue of uncertainty. An argument is made that although professionals are expected to be certain and to possess a font of knowledge on which to draw in their work, it is possible that learning to tolerate uncertainty makes a better professional, especially when the work involves dealing with people and children. This chapter mostly focuses on how research is commonly thought to be done and the results of deviating from these well-worn paths. Questions on the expert role of the professional will also be dealt with. Chapter 5 locates this discussion in the context of my own professional training and first few years of practice, with particular reference to my involvement with Geoffrey and his family. Chapter 6 explores how some of Bion's theories support the above thoughts and ways of practice.

1. WHICH VOICE CAN BE USED IN THIS WRITING?

I am conscious of a distaste which I feel towards something which can be termed as a style of writing. The tone of the writing may be expected to depend on the subject of the writing. And yet, I argue that the manner in which the book is written also contributes to the subject. There is a personal ingredient in this writing as I seek from this style the space and the voice to express some reflections, which are sometimes ignored, and then sometimes returned to in different moments. I am looking for the genuineness of this voice to appeal to the readers and induce them to lend a sympathetic ear (or eye) to what is written.

> I can word it in this way. *What is most personal is most general.* There have been times when in talking with students or staff, or in my writing, I have expressed myself in ways so personal that I have felt that I was expressing an attitude which it was probable no one else could understand, because it was so uniquely my own.... I have almost invariably found that the very feeling which has seemed to me most private, most personal and hence most incomeprehensible by others, has turned out to be an expression for which there is a resonance in many other people. It has led me to believe that what is most personal and unique in each one of us is probably the very element which would, if it were shared or expressed, speak most deeply to others (Rogers, 2001, p. 26).

Carl Rogers writes about this as "a learning which has been most rewarding, because it makes me feel so deeply akin to others" (ibid.). His words express my intention, to write with a style that is genuine, that will appeal to the readers' genuineness and help them find themselves in the relevant parts of the writing. This is not a modest aim, I know, and I also know that by laying bare and specific this aim, I may expose myself to various criticisms, one of which may be that I am trying to over-reach. Perhaps I am taking too big a bite to be able to chew and digest properly. Other persons have told me that I am brave in my writing and I have found that hard to understand. I have also been told that I ought to be prepared to defend myself. But against what, or whom? Can what I am saying be threatening to anyone, who might attack what is perceived as an attack? Or might I be accused of wasting time on a topic which is not useful?

> This is how it should be done: Lodge yourself on a stratum, experiment with the opportunities it offers, find an advantageous place on it, find potential movements of deterritorialisation, possible lines of flight, experience them, produce flow conjunctions here and there, try out continuums of intensities segment by segment, have a small plot of new land at all times (Deleuze and Guattari, 1987, p. 161).

Following Deleuze and Guattari's advice, this space and time to experiment was used with the content and manner of the book. It is important to emphasise, however, that this is not done just for its own sake, but for the sake of something that I felt strongly about. If called upon to defend myself, then the genuineness of my reasons was intended to convince – that would be my plot of land in which I would 'reterritorialise' in Deleuzian terms (1987) – that would be my base from where I stand. Finally I was going to be allowed to ask those "complex questions that people often go into psychology to understand better" (Hollway, 1994, p. 1).

However, when asked the dreaded question regarding the subject of my research was asked, I many times fumbled for an answer as there seemed to be so many threads to it that I did not know which one to grab and use as my subject. I often reported the feeling of being lost and bewildered during the four years and had equally often been told that this was the way it should be in the beginning. However, I had also been told, a little less frequently, by persons whom I greatly admire, that they knew the subject of their doctorate work only after it had been done. My supervisor was one of these persons and he encouraged me to keep holding on although I kept getting more and more confused and also not a little frightened. Each time I thought that I was getting closer to pinning down my topic and could start writing a literature review, a methodology chapter and make some kind of data collection. And each time, I was invited and encouraged to read and take an interest in a different, though in some way related, area. I got upset many times during this process and constantly saw myself as going through various setbacks, never emerging as a winner, but on the contrary, finding myself having regressed each time.

I felt empathy with the character Neo in the film *The Matrix*, when this character discovered that everything he thought he knew, everything he had taken for granted, like the very chair he was sitting on, everything which kept him going, was simply an illusion which he was quickly being stripped of. When given a choice whether to continue in his blissful ignorance or to have an awareness of the illusion in which he lived, Neo chose the latter and went through a rude awakening which was so upsetting that he could not take it physically and psychologically. He had convulsions, went through some kind of heart attack, and also vomited distressingly.

Although I did not experience the same physical reactions, I was conscious of a growing mental distress which I did not feel that I could handle. That feeling of being suspended in a kind of nothingness, of having the ground slowly removed from under my feet and then watching my trainee colleagues grow in their confidence as psychologists affected me. I was never very confident in the first place and I was being encouraged to let this 'lack of confidence' grow and develop. Other psychologists also experienced this confusion and saw it as part of the process (Mellor, 1998). "The sense that the real is relatively stable, determinate, and therefore knowable and predictable" (Law, 2006, p. 144) is replaced by a sense of the "overwhelming, excessive, energetic, a set of undecided potentialities, and an ultimately undecidable flux" (ibid.).

This section aims to explore the assumptions underlying research and the reality which it seeks to uncover. The uncertain and undecided will be tentatively seen in a more positive light with a view to its possible uses in research and professional practice.

2. HOW WE LEARNT WHAT RESEARCH WAS

The formal, scientific research process can be visualised as a straight and narrow path from which it is perilous to deviate as there are booby-traps and hidden pitfalls on the wayside. These traps are called biases and the researcher is taught to watch out and avoid them in order to satisfy two main conditions: reliability and validity. The research questions should be written down very clearly so that the best possible methodology to get at the true answers to those research questions can be found. When the correct methodology is at hand, then its rules ought to be adhered to and meticulous note taken of its limitations. Extraneous variables ought to be controlled as much as is possible and the results should be clinically precise. The fact that social science research does not take place in a laboratory is considered to be unfortunate and everything is to be done so as to counteract this disadvantage in the study. The research needs to be reproducible and also as neat as possible, so that any person reading one's report can carry out the *exact same actions* as those written in the report and come up with *exactly the same results*. If this is not the case, then the steps were either not written clearly, or not exactly followed, or there was something else which polluted the research. Something like the researcher herself perhaps, as the involvement of the person is considered to be a bias. Discrepant data, such as personality factors, are done away with (Schön, 2000, p. 45).

It may now be quite obvious to the reader that I do not subscribe to this ideology of how research is done. I agree with Hollway and Jefferson (2001) that real life is more complex and subtle than scientific research can hope to comprehend and that different perspectives are needed to appreciate this complexity.

> Research is only a more formalised and systematic way of knowing about people, but in the process it seems to have lost much of the subtlety and

> complexity that we use, often as a matter of course, in everyday knowing. We need to bring some of this everyday subtlety into the research process (Hollway and Jefferson, 2001, p. 3).
>
> As Josselson (1995: 32) puts it: 'when we aggregate people, treating diversity as error variable, in search of what is common to all, we often learn about what is true of no one in particular' (ibid., p. 8).

However, for quite a while, I was not aware that there were other ways of researching. Whenever I was asked to complete a questionnaire, I sometimes tried to soul-search so that I could be sure of giving the researcher as true and as genuine an answer as possible. It rarely happened that I was satisfied with the result. Billig et al. (1988) write about "the discovery that people might agree to two questionnaire items, which appear at first sight inconsistent.... One might wish to know how respondents interpret these items, and whether they give a reasoned justification which explains away the seeming inconsistency" (p. 21).

In conducting research to complete the dissertation as part of my undergraduate degree, I administered three hundred questionnaires to tourists and locals in order to assess the occurrence of the actor-observer bias between people of different nationalities. By the end of it, I was convinced that, although my research was valid and reliable, I was nowhere near to getting the kind of understanding that I had wanted of the situation. Originally, I had wanted to get an understanding of the attitudes of the people I questioned. Through operationalising the research questions, they were converted into questions about a bias covered in a social psychology module which I dutifully decided was my main objective. However, the few qualitative questions inserted on the back page of my Likert scale questionnaire yielded more interesting 'juicy' insights about the issue than the long list of character traits on which respondents had to rate their own perceptions. Later, in a presentation on dissertations organised by the university, the latter was what I focussed most on and the audience seemed to identify with such results.

When it came to writing my dissertation for my Masters degree, I was the last person in my cohort to decide what I wanted to focus on. My supervisor took pity on me and asked me what it was which I was interested in. He gave me a few pointers which I took as leading and researched children's perceptions of their own academic performance. I fumbled around a bit more until my tutor told me that I had to sit down and do this, this and this, that my dissertation was not going to change the world and perhaps I should just start and do it. I felt relieved when I had something to do, and got on board with my project and wrote a very good piece of work. It was a case where I panicked because I found myself in what Bannister (1981 in Mellor, 1998) calls the circumspection phase of a creativity cycle, where "...we are bound by no rules and where our minds may and should wander happily ... it is the time when we fantastize, erect preposterous questions, and propose nonsensical answers ... [using] humour, poetry, daydreaming and the wildest kind of speculative argument ... [until we] begin to see the kind of question we want to ask" (Bannister, p. 192–193 in Mellor, p. 460). Owing to constraints of time (this was practically only meant to be a long essay at the end of a very stressful year of professional training), I appreciated my tutor helping me out. It was my own stress at my perceived lack of decisiveness which urged him to give me a 'nudge' in the right direction.

3. NEW WAYS OF CONDUCTING RESEARCH

I knew that the PhD was a much bigger project and that it would take a lot more time. However, I had not bargained for the kind of supervision which I got. My doctorate supervisor resisted every attempt which in retrospect, I realise that I must have made to get him to tell me what to do. Even when I tried to pin myself down to something, he would gently insist on me not pinning myself down just yet and leaving me suspended for a while because he believed that I would find what I needed. My supervisor reflected back to me what he believed were my thoughts about big ideas. Whenever he mentioned them, I always visualised the word big in capital letters and felt that I had a purpose in the doctorate, especially as the 'BIG IDEAS' concerned my practice.

When we once met for a tutorial, I eagerly showed my supervisor what I thought was a good chunk of a chapter of the eventual thesis. He read it all and expressed his liking of what and how I wrote, and then proceeded to point out one specific sentence saying, "This could become a great chapter…" I think I must have stared at him, dumbfounded, for a couple of seconds before I agreed with him, a film of dismay misting my sight. I agreed with him because I could not bear to have him think that I had thought that I had just given him a chapter. I thanked goodness that I had taken it too much for granted that he would realise that this was a chapter and I therefore had not said it out loud specifically. I would never have thought that out of all those pages and all those thousands of words, only one sentence could be seen as potentially being inserted into the thesis. As yet, I had not realised that I was trying to make decisions "without stopping to hear what my automatic self had to say, assuming that my deliberate opinions were all that mattered or even all that existed" (Field, 1990, p. 61).

My upgrade meeting, moreover, had resulted in being told by the readers that I should really pin myself down to having research questions and a methodology, so that I could collect my data and then analyse it. I felt upset following this meeting because I had thought that I *had* been trying to do all this and was being encouraged by my supervisor not to be afraid to think big and wide and to narrow my focus later. I still thought in terms of the right way and wrong way of going about research.

Whenever I pressed too much, my supervisor told me that if the traditional kind of PhD was what I wanted to do, then that is what I should do. However, I kept feeling that the supervision was offering me something and that I might refuse it in favour of the well-worn tracks of 'normal research' in which people knew what they were doing. This would be a missed opportunity if I did not take it on board. In fact, I had not yet realised that this feeling of being suspended came with the research, partly because nowhere is such a phase described as existing, important and crucially necessary to any bit of research worth mentioning. Mellor (1998) writes about method courses and books not seeming to help, "and all the while I was in the thick of practice and thinking about practice" (Mellor, 1998, p. 459). He found Bannister to validate this position when he writes,

> One of the most notable omissions from papers and books on research methodology is any indication of how the researcher is supposed to *think*.... The central issue of how questions are formulated, how we choose, fantasize about, create, uncover, and personally explore ... is almost totally neglected ... the ratio of *thinking time* to *experimental time* is often ludicrously short ... (Bannister, 1981, p. 192, *emphasis as original*, in Mellor, 1998, p. 460).

Law (2006) also writes that it may be impossible to qualify as a social scientist without following courses on research methods and that national recognition of social science courses require the inclusion of the teaching of quantitative and qualitative methods, "though many students and teachers dislike such courses and find their content to be at best marginally relevant to the research process" (p. 4). Smith (2006) quotes Sayer (1994) who compares the importance given in social science courses to the narrow sense of methods "'with the blithe disregard of questions of how we conceptualise, theorise and abstract. ("Never mind the concepts, look at the techniques" might be the slogan)'" (p. 160).

What was helpful in all this was that I never stopped writing. I wrote about my thoughts and about my experiences at work with the children and their families. I wrote about how I felt not knowing what to do my PhD on and how I sometimes thought it was going to be about something and then thought about something else. I wrote about my confusion and my uncertainty and many times found myself writing about my studies and work at the same time. This pleased me because I felt that my one unchanged aim, which was to base my research on my work, was still something which I did not let down and which did not let me down. I did not want my research to be seen as removed from my practice, and yet I specifically wanted it to be an academic piece of work.

When I started reading Joanna Field (1990), Wendy Hollway (1994, 2001) and Wilfred Bion (1994), I realised that other people had written about not being ok with their thoughts. Other people had actually managed to capture their thoughts and write about them in ways which described their complexity (Field, 1990). It was fine to have conflict and confusing messages within oneself (Hollway, 1994, 2001). There were actually reasons for being in such a state and it was only by learning to live with it that I could turn it to my advantage for my studies and to the advantage of the children and people with whom I work (Bion, 1994). Thus, I realised that when I put my researcher's lens on, those thoughts which I used to think were asides were actually being brought to the forefront and I would find valid reasons for things that I wanted said or written, and also things that I heard being said and read on paper. The possibility that I was seeing my confusion and uncertainty as 'asides' started to occur to me, and consequently the result was that they were given a more prominent place in my thinking. I also learnt to question what was left unsaid and unwritten and how both reinforced the other. Having daily discussions with my partner about Derrida's ideas on the undecided were equally helpful. This shift in perspective started taking place haltingly and with numerous regressions. It was as though I was lifting stones in a country path: everything looked smooth and apparent, but when the stones were lifted, it could be seen that underneath teemed with life. I was taking the apparent and peeking beneath it, thus uncovering a whole new world.

I was reminded about something which we learnt during our undergraduate psychology course in a credit aptly called Helping Skills. Thoughts, feelings and impressions about the here and now come under the category of immediacy (Egan, 1994) where the therapist would bring to the forefront feelings which came out of the therapeutic process. The expression of such thoughts and feelings would be used to aid the therapeutic relationship. It is about the ability to discuss with a client where the two stand in the overall relationship with each other and is especially useful in situations where the client experiences difficulty in interpersonal relationships and the therapist can provide empathic feedback on the interpersonal relationship between them. Immediacy "is difficult…because the helper, without becoming self-preoccupied and without 'psyching out' the client, needs to be aware of what is happening in the relationship and have enough psychological distance to catch difficult moments as they happen and react to them without trivialising the helping process" (Egan, 1994, p. 190).

Using immediacy required an almost physical action of turning my focus inward, and consequently broadening it. When Joanna Field first noticed trees, she writes that she literally felt she was "spreading the arms of my awareness towards the trees, letting myself flow around them and feed on the delicacy of their patterns till their intricacies became part of my being…" (Field, 1990, p. 74). It was a kind of exploration, a learning process, in which I was encouraging my awareness to discover these inner subtle promptings and to give them time, weight and space.

4. PUTTING THERAPY IN RESEARCH AND WORK-RELATED ISSUES

Perhaps the introduction of the above therapeutic note is not as random and sporadic as it may look. I had learnt a lot of helpful counselling skills during my undergraduate course and became quite adept at using empathy and probing in my training sessions with other students. I was also encouraged, during these four years, to be reflective and to analyse myself in retrospect using various ways and means. However, I had not realised, up till this moment when I am looking back to see how I learnt about Immediacy as a skill, that I was still using it in my work with people. Furthermore, I had not realised that I was also using it with myself. In a very coincidental and unsystematic way, I would sometimes realise that I was mulling over something and trying to bring it out to the open.

> I get a picture and then there is a niggling feeling. It is very easy to ignore it and stay with what is at face value. But I've learnt that that feeling is the truest of the truths about that picture and every time I've ignored it, it's haunted me. The best way that I can describe it is to ask you to imagine a computer screen. The computer is turned on and there is a picture there for you to see. At the bottom right hand corner is a little group of pixels, called a spot, which is bleeping and changing colour. As you stare at the picture you do not notice it, but after a while, in the aftermath of the feeling of the whole picture, it calls your attention. At first you do not realise what is irritating your peace of mind,

> or of vision. But gradually, you are able to tear yourself away from the whole picture and you realise that there's something which does not quite fit in. You decide here whether to ignore it in favour of the whole sensation, or to give it your whole attention. You drag your mouse on it and the arrow changes to a pointed hand as soon as it touches the bleeping spot. Aha! There's something there! Click on it and from that spot another window opens with a mine of information, or rather, a mine of questions which, even unanswered, give another perspective to the situation – perhaps another frame of mind. This is what I mean, I suppose, by intuition (Journal: December, 2002).

> The function…can be likened to the 'pause' and 'slow-motion' buttons on a DVD player, with the added 'zoom' possibility to whatever can be seen on the screen. Its aim is to reflect and analyse, using such tools as I can find in my readings, the motion picture in which I have an active participative role… I liken the process to the pause and slow-motion functions of a DVD player, because that is what I am doing with the issues I write about, and then taking a close look at them as though through a magnifying glass (Conversion paper, 2004).

These attempts at explaining I later found presented in a more coherent and structured manner in Damasio's *The feeling of what happens* (1999). This author writes that it is "only along with the advent of a sense of self do feelings become known to the individual having them" (p. 36). Thus, particular states of feeling of which we become conscious do not begin with the consciousness but rather some time before. Damasio maintains that although "consciousness must be present if feelings are to influence the subject having them beyond the immediate here and now" (p. 37), still "the biological machinery underlying emotion is not dependent on consciousness" (p. 43). He cites an empirical test carried out in his laboratory which clearly showed that one does not need to be conscious of the inducer of an emotion to be able to experience that emotion and claims that "we are about as effective at stopping an emotion as we are at preventing a sneeze. We can try to prevent the expression of an emotion, and we may succeed in part but not in full" (p. 49).

What Damasio (1999) is describing fits in with my thoughts. It started to become a systematic exercise in which I would notice that something did not quite fit and then try to focus on it to bring it to the forefront where I could attend to what it was (rather than try to delete it because of its lack of fit). The technical allegories sometimes helped but I still only had a vague sense of where I was heading and kept feeling discouraged each time this became painfully apparent. One such example occurred following my meeting with other research students where I outlined my study. I appreciated the discussion which they had, especially as two quite opposing ideas came out from the group. However, while I was packing my overheads and notes, I asked one of the tutors what he thought about my presentation. He replied that he still did not know what I wanted to get out of my study.

I remember myself wincing at this. Persons I esteem greatly and appreciate for their support were concerned about my research – should I not listen to them and choose a topic of research would be *chosen* first and foremost, and then write research questions and choose a tried and tested methodology which would best serve the ends of the research questions? A friend of mine who is a dentist with a strong background in scientific research interested himself in my study when I told him that I was reading a PhD (he had just finished his). When I started explaining, his expression changed; he looked puzzled and asked "but that's not reproducible!" I tried to explain that generalising results is not always the first aim in research and that I was after a more subtle 'truth' – his puzzlement turned to shock and concern "but that's not scientific!"

Such interaction happened frequently with different people, in various professions. I was always frightened following such debate. It was comforting, later, to come across Smith's (2003) paper, where he terms this kind of debate as "here indeed were students thinking with each other" (Smith, 2003, p. 321). Then, I still thought that there was a right way and a wrong way and that I was risking it. Law (2006) sums up the argument in the following manner: "If you want to understand reality properly then you need to follow the methodological rules. Reality imposes those rules on us. If we fail to follow them, we will end up with substandard knowledge, knowledge that is distorted or does not represent what it purportedly describes" (p. 5). Although I had read and studied about the predominance of the scientific method being largely a result of the weight that medical professions had, I had not yet seen myself in this picture. I did not realise that this was what I was questioning and that the concerns expressed by the above tutor and others were genuine attempts not to let me stray from the straight and narrow path. I was still thinking that I had strayed beyond redemption and not that I was discovering my own path (based on many others before me).

Because of the predominance of the scientific method, do I need to make sure that I adequately defend and justify what I am doing? Hollway (1994) does so, in ways that even the most generous person must interpret as defensive. It cannot really be helped – we have grown up with this idea and because we are doing something different, then we must argue why it needs to be so. Rorty (1989) expresses this as the distinction between normal and abnormal discourse, where the former "is that which is conducted within an agreed-upon set of conventions about what counts as a relevant contribution, what counts as answering a question, what counts as having a good argument for that answer or a good criticism for it. Abnormal discourse is what happens when someone joins in the discourse who is ignorant of these conventions or who sets them aside" (p. 320). Rorty explains that one only reaches abnormal discourse through the discourse which is normal and says that the difference between what the two terms represent may be "purely one of familiarity" (p. 321) rather than something more deeply universal. Perhaps this is the way things are at present – that it never crosses anyone's mind to question why a person has chosen the scientific method of research. Perhaps in the future, I will find it just as natural to question my dentist friend with the same puzzled and shocked air that he questioned me with: "but what you are doing is scientific!"

5. THE SCIENTIFIC NATURE OF INQUIRY

What might further shock my friend would be 'evidence' which convinces him that even 'scientific research' is not as 'scientific' as it would seem. Feyerabend (1975), who regarded himself as an anarchist, argues convincingly that a historical scientific method does not exist, and thus, science does not deserve its privileged status in Western society. He names numerous examples of scientific accomplishments which traditionally owe their success to non-scientific elements and believed that there is no justification for valuing scientific claims over claims by other ideologies. Science is, according to Feyerabend, obsessed with its own mythology and makes claims to truth well beyond its actual capacity. In fact, Feyerabend insisted that law-and-order science inhibits progress and that the only principle which does not do this is: *anything goes*.

> For is it not possible that science as we know it today, or a 'search for the truth' in the style of traditional philosophy, will create a monster? Is it not possible that an objective approach that frowns upon personal connections between the entities examined will harm people, turn them into miserable, unfriendly, self-righteous mechanisms without charm or humour? 'Is it not possible,' asks Kierkegaard, 'that my activity as an objective [or critico-rational] observer of nature will weaken my strength as a human being?' I suspect the answer to many of these questions is affirmative and I believe that a reform of the sciences that makes them more anarchic and more subjective (in Kierkegaard's sense) is urgently needed (Feyerabend, 1975, internet source).

Midgley (1992) also explores the idea that science is salvation and says that increasing technicality and specialisation have promised to serve "the general need for understanding, and whatever spiritual needs lie behind it. The promise...has built up a strong emotive and romantic conception of 'science' as a spiritual power" (p. 2). Indeed, science is seen as a universally important ideal, a value which all should strive to nurture; it is the "duty and hope of us all to be in some way scientific" (p. 3). Wellington (2000), in fact, calls "a persistent illusion" the notion that there is something called the scientific method which scientists follow and which should be adopted by education research. "It remains a mystery to me why those who work in education should attempt to aspire towards science when scientific methods, processes and codes of conduct at best are unclear and at worst lack the objectivity, certainty, logicality and predictability which are falsely ascribed to them." (p. 14). When discussing how science ought to be presented to young persons in school, Wellington insists that the curriculum should not portray science as uncontroversial – being a human activity, it is not as objective as we believe.

Rowbottom and Aiston (2006) begin their paper on the myth of 'scientific method' by quoting Popper saying that it does not exist. What they term as the outdated orthodox positivist account still continues to dominate educational research, and further judge such an account as unrealistic and irrelevant (quoting Carr and Kemmis, 1986, p. 71), and divisive and detrimental to social science. In fact, the authors argue that a widely used text book written by Cohen, Manion and Morrison (2003), among others, further serves to perpetuate this system of misrepresentation of science and scientists, which system is "closed, stale and self-referential" (Rowbottom and Aiston, 2006, p. 139). They contend that the claim that there is a natural scientific method is false: "...while we wholeheartedly support the notion of widening the conception of science, we suggest that we should widen it even further, by rejecting the idea of a scientific method, and recognise that good inquiry – rather than 'doing science' – is what really matters" (Rowbottom and Aiston, 2006, p. 138). An echo of Feyerabend (1975) is heard as Rowbottom and Aiston maintain that methodological flexibility is necessary to allow inquiry to flourish, while enforcing "obedience to 'the methods' is just to impede progress, by preventing the exploration of new avenues" (p. 154). In fact, I believe that Rowbottom and Aiston would approve of my 'method' as they suggest that the researcher should be willing to design and craft her very own tools when appropriate and thus liberate herself from 'the dungeon of dogmatism'.

When writing on the same topic in 1983, Carr had also insisted that scientific rationality is not achieved by simply conforming to a set of unambiguous methodological rules and moreover pushes forward the idea that rationality is not to be identified with the exclusion of fallible human judgement (p. 41). Carr (2006) quotes Gadamer who shows "how modern social science has its own 'effective history', how its concepts of 'rationality' and 'objectivity' are internal to a tradition, and hence, how social scientific knowledge is only as 'rational' or 'objective' as the historically rooted prejudices that this tradition has bequeathed" (p. 430). Medawar (1967) terms the idea that science is equated with facts and humanity with ideas as "one of the shabby genteelisms that bolster up the humanist's self esteem" (p. 114). He sees this as an attempt to keep science 'below stairs' as it is conceived to be associated with trade – Medawar writes profusely about such popular misconceptions of scientific thought.

Many authors draw upon Aristotle to emphasise how he originally thought that intuition is the first apprehension of anything which greets the mind. Billington (2000), in particular, argues that his writing is "a means of re-engaging with [his] own 'knowing' or intuition" (Billington, 2000, p. 116), which, he claims, is still valid as a methodology. The scientific knowing which Billington is after is informed by 'intuition' and 'intelligence', both words being interchangeable for Aristotle (Billington here cites the editor's footnote in Aristotle, 1976, p. 211). Billington's argument is that this 'knowing' cannot be contained in a model of human science which has a medical materialism as its base: "For such a model lacks the capacity to hold the dialectical co-existence, interaction and inter-dependency of the infinite complexity of human conditions, as well as its simultaneous crushing simplicity" (Billington, 2000, p. 117). Rather than remain blind to the economic and political processes which underlie states of knowing, Billington attempts to adopt scientific positions which maintain their alertness to, and question, such processes. In searching for his own knowing, Billington searches for science.

> I argue that it is possible to declare with more certainty that the application of a merely positivist science towards human abilities tells us only a little about John, Gary, Mary, Peter or James for it tells us only a little about their human experience, their intelligence and qualities. It is by keeping alive stories of human experience which can recognise such qualities that further resistance to the pathologising tendency will be found (ibid., p. 120).

Law (2006), in fact, draws upon Latour and Woolgar's (1986) work to explore the reason why it is not obvious that 'inscription devices' produce not only the statements about reality but also the realities themselves. To provide a pragmatic explanation, these inscription devices are what convert what is non-tracelike into trace-like form. A technology or an instrument could be examples of such devices. In practice, it is "the process of *making* particular kinds of relations in an experimental and instrumental set-up, and turning these into traces" (Law, 2006, p. 29). Latour and Woolgar (1986) are quoted:

> We do not wish to say that facts do not exist nor that there is no such thing as reality. In this simple sense our position is not relativist. Our point is that 'out-there-ness' is the *consequence* of scientific work rather than its *cause*. We therefore wish to stress the importance of timing (p. 182 in Law, 2006, p. 29).

The end result is that this timing covers up the traces of how reality is constituted. Law (2006) argues that as the object of scientific practice is to make unqualified statements about reality, these statements have formed part of the routine by turning them into taken-for-granted assumptions. The processes in which the statements are produced are also deleted so that the reality which supports it is standardised.

> But it is the 'subjective' and the 'personal' that disappears first. The traces and the statements in the laboratory are used 'in such a way that all the statements were seen to relate to something outside of, or beyond, the reader's or author's subjectivity' (1986, 84).
>
> This deletion of subjectivity is crucial. In natural and social science research statements about objects in the world are supposed to issue from the world itself, examined in the proper way by means of proper methods, and not from the person who happens to be conducting the experiment. If this is not achieved, then independence and anteriority are not achieved either. If the scientist appears in her text, if she appears as a person, then this undermines any statement about reality (Law, 2006, p. 36).

What then happens is that the scientific statements become an object in themselves and thus take on a life of their own, so that they are no longer seen as products of discussion and debate, but are what cause, and also settle, such discussion and debate. Reality is attributed more to the object and less to the statement about the object. "Consequently an inversion takes place: the object becomes the reason why the statement was made in the first place" (Woolgar and Latour, 1986, p. 177 in Law, 2006, 37). The result is a sense of a world that is assumed to be independent of and prior to scientific attempts to know it.

It thus seems to be a question about what kind of knowledge and knowing one is after. If the aim is to establish an element of undeniable truth, then one has no choice but to isolate the event being studied and make sure that all the influencing factors are accounted for and controlled. The result will eventually establish a causation or correlation of some kind. However, the truth which is found has to be, because of all these checks and controls, very small and far removed from the original quest for understanding which prompts most people to take an interest in people and study psychology. How can the previously mentioned "complexity and subtlety" be controlled? – when one controls it, it instantly loses its complexity and becomes artificial. People, as often mournfully noted in basic undergraduate research books, do not produce their natural behaviour in a laboratory or some other controlled environment, so we must get our hands dirty in the field. Since people are complex thinking human beings, they will not fit into a neat array of pigeonholes (Parker, Georgaca, Harper, McLaughlin, and Stowell-Smith, 1995). Hollway (1994) reiterates: "I wanted to study psychology because I wanted to understand people (that phrase has come to sound trite and naïve, but I think it needs to be reclaimed for serious psychology)…. I am reminded that what I know bears little or no resemblance to psychology as a discipline. I still do not know how to respond to those who assume that psychology has taught me to understand people. Except that by running the risk of doing an unorthodox Ph.D., and by writing this book, I hope to show how a psychology which understands people is possible" (Hollway, 1994, p. 3). The small kernel of truth found by scientific study does not help us in our work with people: "Complexity, instability, and uncertainty are not removed or resolved by applying specialised knowledge to well-defined tasks" (Schön, 2000, p. 19).

So much has the study of psychology been perceived as removed from reality, that I felt it incumbent on me to title this section the introduction of the element of therapy into psychology. "Psychologists generally proceed with their work without stopping to reflect on the basic assumptions that underlie what they are doing" (Tolman, 1994, p. 23). If the word therapy is mentioned then there ought to be no confusion about the search to understand people. It seems as though the word therapy has taken on the interesting bits of psychology and the latter has been left with the dry 'dead' bits of unrelated knowledge. Thus, even if I were to take what is considered to be the softer option in research and to conduct qualitative research, still there would be the necessity of seeing how such data could be analysed. "The more unstructured it is, the greater the anxiety that it is going to be impossible to analyse rigorously" (Hollway, 1994, p. 21) Coding, classifying and sorting come at hand and whole chunks of speech or writing is chopped and re-arranged to fit certain categories. There are even computer programmes which carry this tedious task out for the researcher.

However, even here, "the result was unsatisfactory in several respects…it made me realise that what I was trying to understand was a complex whole…by separating them I was doing violence to the relations between categories…. The relations were best demonstrated by the integrity of someone's experience…I realised that these shouldn't be chopped up in the interest of methodological 'rigour' which was more characteristic of naturalism" (Hollway, 1982, p. 257 in Hollway, 1994, p. 21). It seems that unless one specifically makes it clear that the aim is to gain an understanding of experience as a whole, the chances are that educational psychology is becoming a discipline and practice which is made up of "'pieces' of dead knowledge" (Billington, 2000, p. 113). Is the only way to prevent this from happening to be the inclusion of therapy in practice? Is this the way of ensuring that the interest in understanding and, yes why not, caring for people is safeguarded? Perhaps this is an answer.

6. THE CRISIS OF CONFIDENCE

This is the title of Schön's first chapter in his book *The Reflective Practitioner* (2000), in which he outlines the apparent disillusionment that society has undergone with regards to professionals and professionalism. Professionals are accepted as experts and to *know* with certainty, thus never in a quandary. However, for several reasons, some of which are discussed below, the performance of professionals has not lived up to the standards which the aura of the professionals has set. This has resulted in a crisis of confidence in the professional status. Should professionals be certain or is it permissible that they can be uncertain? If the latter were possible, then being a professional would not be about being an expert first and foremost. Perhaps the acknowledgement of the expert role as lodged within the persons *receiving* the services of the professionals, as opposed to *giving* them, might go a long way towards meeting this crisis of confidence. The chapter title seemed to sum up my own worries with regards to my work: do I have qualms because I am naïve and inexperienced (which is what I have been told is the case)? Or do I have qualms because having qualms and consequently being reflective about one's work ensures the good quality of that work? Would I still have qualms if I studied more and knew more? This subsection aims to explore the idea that professionals are in possession of expert knowledge.

I was once part of a working group whose aim was to contribute to a document commissioned by the Commissioner for Children. The document was written, re-written and revised several times and the moment came for our names to be written near the title. A discussion came up because one of the members of this group was a mother (not a professional or 'expert') and she modestly said that perhaps she ought not to have her name included as she was not a professional. Instant outcries from everybody refuted her suggestion that she had not really contributed anything, especially as her attendance to the meetings was exemplary and she had often taken on the role of keeping minutes (were we allocating her, the only non-professional, to secretary status?) When I thought about this later, I realised that most of the professionals present in the working group were not parents. Although the group member who introduced herself as a parent lacked the training and practice which the rest of the group received to become caring professionals, we lacked something which I believed was equally, if not more, important. We lacked the experience of becoming parents and of maintaining such a role. However, it seems that while we have to remind ourselves of the importance of parents as it is very often taken for granted, the importance of the professional is emblazoned in society and we come across it in almost every activity. Perhaps the way forward is to see the expert in non-professionals and to see the uncertainty in professionals.

This also depends on the context: in some circles and geographical areas, being a professional, and being considered as such, is given a lot of importance. One is really considered to be the expert; as Schön (2000) writes, professionals claim to extraordinary knowledge and "in return, we grant professionals extraordinary rights and privileges" (p. 4). But do they really have such extraordinary knowledge? Can they be where all positive developments in this world, and beyond it, originate? Are professionals the persons on whom society, and the rest of the living and non-living world, is to depend? Schön (2000) gives several examples of how discoveries and inventions which professionals have come up with have gone wrong. They are the results of people believing that they *know* everything. The autonomy which professionals enjoy, as society relies on their code of ethics, has been exploited and misused repeatedly and it seems that professionals cannot be trusted by society to act for the good of the world and humanity.

When it comes to the difficulties experienced by children, the very systems created by professionals aimed at helping children sometimes serve to propagate the problem, to delay dealing with the problem, or to make it even worse for the affected persons to get help. These shortcomings are coming out in the open and "scientists and scientifically trained professionals found themselves in the unfamiliar role of the villain" (Schön, 2000, p. 10). Situations which professionals are being asked to 'fix' are becoming more complex and complicated and they find themselves "called upon to perform tasks for which they have not been educated" (ibid., p. 14). While seeking to protect the aura and mysticism surrounding the expert, professionals could be shocked by the current vogue of accountability required from them. Courses which train professionals are continuously being evaluated and sometimes regarded as falling short of what is required to train a professional. Following their professional training, many are the psychologists who say that the real world is nowhere near to what they have been taught – and this is training which is specifically called professional and is perceived as worth more than a normal Masters degree. In fact, it costs much more also.

Training courses in the helping professions everywhere compartmentalise people in such a way that the complexity which is people may be left out. While covering learning difficulties, emotional and behavioural difficulties, parental involvement etc., the illusion seems to be created that as we compartmentalise the course, for the sake of convenience, thus we also compartmentalise our conceptions of children and their families. Compartmentalisation is done for the sake of practicality – as kind of shorthand which is manageable. However, as explained above in Law's (2006) argument on how the traces which produce reality are covered up, we tend to forget that the reason for which the holistic person is categorised and compartmentalised into bits is for the sake of convenience. These bits of courses take a life of their own, and become objects which we attempt to manage, forgetting that, through their very existence, it is they who are managing our thoughts.

When, as newly qualified practitioners we face families and children in school, we end up feeling swamped by the invasion of the dynamics, which are so intricately co-dependent and interrelated that one cannot possibly separate them, convenient though it may be. In Chapter 10 the way society is divided so that piece-meal support is provided to situations of children in need will be explored. However, here the difficulty faced by the practitioner is that she is thrown on herself and needs to call on different kinds of resources to handle situations. "I argue here that, had I relied solely on my professional training I would not have been able to acknowledge the complex nature of James' capacity for thinking, feeling and communication so clearly for training had not encouraged consideration of one's own anxieties as a legitimate resource" (Billington, 2000, p. 104). This latter point is crucial in that it ties up to something already previously hinted at: the importance of being aware of one's own state of being as possibly interacting and contributing to one's intervention with 'a case'.

This kind of involvement was referred to by Schön as the choice of the professional to work in the 'swampy lowlands'. "They deliberately involve themselves in messy but crucially important problems and, when asked to describe their methods of inquiry, they speak of experience, trial and error, intuition, and muddling through" (Schön, 2000, p. 43). This oft-quoted sentence has been used by many a professional who has appreciated the recognition of muddling through as a legitimate method of inquiry. "The reality was painful and messy. Re-mapping of this nature is rarely an isolated academic exercise: it happens deep in Schön's (1983) swampy lowlands of professional practice – where yesterday's sense of direction can often be lost in the struggle to survive in the quicksand of today's imperatives" (Hunt, C., 2001, p. 283). Also, "I was in Schön's (1983) 'swampy lowland ... of confusing messes' (p. 42), 'working without rules in order to find out the rules of what you've done' (Appignanesi and Garrett, 1995, p. 50) (Mellor, N., 2001, p. 465).

CONCLUSION

This chapter questioned the apparent certainty and stability with which both research methods *and* what they attempt to study seem to be invested. A case is made for the possibility of research and professional practice to be uncertain. This argument will be referred to and expanded further in the next two chapters. The following quote from Law seems a fitting conclusion to the arguments put forward above:

> I would like to divest concern with method of its inheritance of hygiene. I want to move from the moralist idea that if only you do your methods properly you will lead a healthy research life – the idea that you will discover specific truths about which all reasonable people can at least temporarily agree. I want to divest it of what I will call 'singularity': the idea that indeed there are definite and limited sets of processes, single sets of processes, to be discovered if only you lead a healthy research life. I also want to divest it of a commitment to a particular version of politics: the idea that unless you attend to certain more of less determinate phenomena (class, gender or ethnicity would be examples), then your work has no political relevance. I want to subvert method by helping to remake methods: that are not moralist; that imagine and participate in politics and other forms of the good in novel and creative ways; and that start to do this by escaping the postulate of singularity, and responding creatively to a world that is taken to be composed of an excess of generative forces and relations.
>
> To do this we will need to unmake many of our methodological habits, including: the desire for certainty; the expectation that we can usually arrive at more or less stable conclusions about the way things really are; the belief that as social scientists we have special insights that allow us to see further than others into certain parts of social reality; and the expectations of generality that are wrapped up in what is often called 'universalism'. But first of all we need to unmake our desire and expectation for security (Law, 2006, p. 9).

CHAPTER 5

MEETING GEOFFREY

This chapter concerns my own journey as a professional and also my involvement with Geoffrey. I am narrating these two stories in order to contextualise the issues of uncertainty and insecurity mentioned in the previous chapter. The narrative of my involvement as an educational psychologist with Geoffrey also serves as an example of how certainty and validation of the self is searched for in professional practice.

1. THE FIRST YEAR FOLLOWING PROFESSIONAL TRAINING

As referred to in the previous chapter, I kept finding myself in Schön's (2000) swampy lowlands both in my work as an educational psychologist as well as in my research. Coincidentally, having started my doctorate immediately after my professional training, I began both my professional as well as my academic journeys at the same time. Thus, both went very much hand in hand, and I realised that one was not separate from the other in any respect. I wrote about both, I was given supervision for both, I was anxious and confused about both. To make matters a little more complicated, I went back home after two years away (in which I had one year of practice and doctorate study) and in the meantime, also got married.

While in the United Kingdom, I worked on a part-time basis with an Educational Psychology Service. I believe that one of the reasons for which my application was accepted was that I was very sceptical about the use of psychometric tests to assess children's abilities and needs. Great changes, in terms of magnitude, had taken place in this service as the aims of all the educational psychologists there were to reduce the amount of statementing as it was seen as not the sole answer to children's difficulties. The statement is what may emerge as a result of the intervention of a psychologist who assesses a child and then issues a report in which the quality and amount of support deemed necessary to support a child is stated. The report, or 'advice' is considered, along with other reports and a decision is taken as to whether or how much support can be allocated. One of the controversial issues around statements is that while it apparently helps a child, it may serve to further highlight that child's needs and locate the difficulties more firmly within a child, so that the contribution of the environment to the difficulties may be overlooked. In this service, statementing was not seen as an end in itself, but only as one of the means available (and a very expensive one at that) to an end. Psychometric assessments were regarded as the tools which naturally seemed to lead solely to the issuing of statements. Thus, when the head of service once saw me looking at the few psychometric tests which were available in the service, he earnestly but jokingly urged me to "steel myself" against the temptation to use them. Although I explained that I was contemplating assessing a child with a psychometric test in order to prove to disbelieving teachers that the child was very intelligent, he encouraged me to use curriculum-based or some other assessments instead. I liked the way this head of service believed in what he did and kept adhering to his values instead of giving in to administrative and bureaucratic pressures.

I was placed to work with a team of educational psychologists and had a very small caseload, owing to my working only two days a week. I got on with the team and enjoyed the work. As had happened already in my experience in the United Kingdom, I started to receive feedback from various persons whose impression of me was that I was a very confident and decided person. The fact that I was away from home and trying out so many new things, and possibly also my Mediterranean manners, perhaps gave that impression to persons who did not know me very well. However, after a few months, I asked my senior whether he still thought of me as a secure confident person and he told me that his idea of me had changed in that respect. I had spoken to him about each and every case that I was involved with and checked whether I was doing the right thing and whether I was asking the right questions at every step of the way.

I was being shown and told how the service worked and I kept feeling worried that I was not doing enough for the children that I worked with. I started to think that I had so much to learn about how to be an educational psychologist that I tried to take as much information as possible in order to bring home with me. I photocopied almost every bit of paper that I thought I would not find in at home and kept up the hope that the more files I filled with information, the better a psychologist I would one day become. One day, when I read all that stuff, and knew how to implement it; when I could be more certain of myself, I would become a great psychologist.

When I eventually returned home, I joined the one local school psychology service. I was anxious to perform, to show my mettle and to prove myself. The old insecurities re-emerged. Was I not as prepared to work with children and their families as my colleagues were? The situation verged on the panic-stage when I was almost given a case of school phobia as my first case. It had happened that I had not been directly involved with such a case in my training. When I reluctantly admitted this, my senior told me that he thought that I might prefer to start off with a different case and perhaps take on the next referral of school refusal with some supervision. I agreed and started with my case. It was quite a mortifying ordeal and I did not emerge from it unscathed. I felt totally incompetent and for a while raged against some of my tutors in the professional masters training, who had outlined the merits of the particular slant which our training course had when we told them that we felt very inadequate when compared to trainee educational psychologists in other universities (this is expanded on further in Chapter 10). I had forgotten that the value of our training was that we always saw a child as a child, and not as a case, or a difficulty.

3. MEETING GEOFFREY

Geoffrey's mother and her son came to me for an assessment. I liked the mother and enjoyed the time spent with her six year old son. This was especially so because Geoffrey had presented quite a challenge. He refused to say hello to me during the whole hour while I spoke to his mother and I was at my wits' end to know how I could at least get him to tell me his name. I thought that if only we could exchange two words, their visit would not be in vain. My Journal recounts what happened:

> When Geoffrey and his mother visited me for the first time, he would not speak to me, although he gave me some lovely smiles and giggled at my jokes. After trying to engage with him a few times without success, I did not give him any more attention and spoke mostly with his mother... Towards the end of the visit, I again tried to get him to interact with me beyond looking and smiling and only succeeded because he tried to run away as I pretended to run after him. He dived under the table and sat there and after a moment's hesitation I went in after him, and we both ended up underneath the table, where he allowed me to speak to him and spoke back to me in the same conspiratorial whisper that I had used with him.... These whispers consisted of plans of what to do the next time we met, and thus the groundwork for the next visit was laid (Journal: February, 2004)

I was so elated at what I perceived to be my success with this child that I looked forward to seeing him again. It is not difficult to appreciate and enjoy what validates one's positive self concept and that incident with Geoffrey did exactly that for me. Yet throughout my assessment with Geoffrey, I was uneasy and was made more uncomfortable because I could not understand the reason for this uneasiness. I had the feeling that all was not right and yet Geoffrey's responses to the subtests in the assessments were not raising much concern. His scores were in the lower average range but I was well aware that my psychometric tests were standardised for UK children and that Geoffrey would be expected to get low scores. However, my worry was that, considering what his mother was telling me and how he presented, I expected his scores to be even lower and could not understand how this boy was achieving higher than my expectations. At one point, Geoffrey's mother disclosed to me that he loved food to the extent that he needed to have the biggest portion, bigger than his dad's, and also frequently wanted to have second helpings. She said that at school he asks to eat his lunch much before the bell rings for break-time and said that he is not expected to be hungry because of the large breakfast he has before leaving the house for school.

I clutched at this, like the proverbial drowning man does at a straw, and worried over it. Again I could not tolerate Bannister's (1981 in Mellor, 1998) circumspection phase of the creativity cycle. I still felt that I had to have the answer at hand instead of allowing my mind to 'wander happily'. My argument is that Bannister's deploring that there is no reading on research methodology which indicates how a researcher is supposed to think can also be applied to practice. It seems as though in the work of an educational psychologist, as with the other helping professionals, there is not much time between the presentation of a problem and the expectancy of a solution. Pressure from without *and* from within is felt so that the helping professional comes up with something to 'help' and save the day.

When Geoffrey's mother told me about his seeming obsession with food, I decided that this could be the clue to what was mulling over in my mind and called the mother in the middle of the week, asking her whether she would take Geoffrey to the paediatrician and tell her what she had told me about food. She agreed to do so. I did not let the mother know that my mind instantly thought about Prader-Willi syndrome and that I thought that Geoffrey's craving for food might be one of the symptoms. I was half ashamed of my eagerness and was not sure that I thought of it because I was desperate or whether it was really a possibility which ought to be explored. The excuse I gave to the mother was that I wanted to ensure that Geoffrey was not diabetic. The fact that she told me that the paediatrician had also once thought this about Geoffrey helped me allay my qualms. I did not want to think that I was looking for an easy solution. I wanted to think that I was doing the right thing and that I was being professional.

When the parents next came so that Geoffrey's assessment could be completed, they told me that the paediatrician mentioned the possibility that Geoffrey might need genetic testing because it might be the case that Geoffrey had some sort of syndrome. My heart leapt at this confirmation of my fears – but it was a confirmation of myself - and although the mother said she could not remember the name of the syndrome, I asked her whether it sounded like Prader-Willi, to which she replied yes it did. I could not believe it. I actually felt happiness and tried to mask it with concern (which was genuinely felt, in the midst of all this confusion). I felt vindicated that a doctor, a paediatrician, no less, had the same hypothesis that I had. It was as though the fact that the opinion of this professional (who was firmly established as such) coincided with mine made me more of the kind of professional I thought I should be. The geneticist at the hospital also agreed that Geoffrey could be a candidate for testing and his blood samples were set to France. I wrote profusely about this incident, believing that it would aid me to increase my self-confidence and stand me in good stead the next time I was faced with a child about whom I was not sure. I believed that the next time, I would not let a paediatrician tell the mother about the possibility of her child having Prader-Willi. I would do so myself. This time, I felt that I had chickened out – next time I would not.

Imagine my shock and surprise when the genetic results emerged which said that Geoffrey had tested negatively for Prader-Willi syndrome and also for Fragile-X syndrome. I accompanied the parents to the hospital to receive the results and the doctor asked me what Geoffrey's IQ was. When I said it was within the low average range, the reply was that children with Prader-Willi syndrome had IQ which was lower than average and had they known that Geoffrey's IQ was within average range they could have ruled out the possibility of him having Prader-Willi. Again, we were back to square one. By that time, I had got over my triumph at having suspected the same condition as a paediatrician. I felt intense relief that Geoffrey did not have a syndrome which would cause him and his family great difficulties to cope. His parents had also happier, less worried looks on their faces and we discussed behavioural strategies how Geoffrey's craving for food could be managed. It became a behavioural difficulty.

4. SHARING UNCERTAINTY WITH GEOFFREY'S MOTHER

Throughout this whole incident, a friendship was slowly forming between Geoffrey's parents and my husband and myself. Since Geoffrey ran so shy of new persons and places, the assessment took place either at my home or at his, and this, together with the fact that we knew Geoffrey's aunt a little, made our relationship with each other deeper than the normal psychologist-client relationship. The professional and ethical issues regarding this will be discussed further in Chapter 7. Every now and then we called each other and friendships formed out of acquaintances.

During such conversations, I would ask about how Geoffrey was doing and the mother would clue me in to the latest news. I kept wondering whether I had done all that I could to help them, feeling certain that a 'better' psychologist might have found the key. Geoffrey's mother once told me how worried she sometimes got about her husband, who spends all afternoon with Geoffrey to help him with his homework. Geoffrey hates doing this, especially the extra work necessary for revision, and he gives his father a hard time. Geoffrey's mother said that she sometimes fears for her husband's health because he has to be so patient with Geoffrey. Although I had met with the head of school and also wrote a report to be given to Geoffrey's teacher with recommendations of how best to help Geoffrey with his learning, still things were quite hard for him.

> Yesterday Sylvia, Geoffrey's mother, called and I spoke to her a little bit and then inquired after his exams. She said he was upset because the teacher took him out of the room during exams without preparation and without informing her. We spoke a little about why Geoffrey finds it so hard to learn what school teaches. And I felt – again – so worried and fearful about my past assessment. Geoffrey's scores hadn't been that bad. But they weren't good. He has a short attention span. Sylvia said that last Friday she just cried and cried with sadness about Geoffrey – she said it couldn't be that he's got nothing wrong – there must be something wrong, maybe ADD or ADHD. Is he so ignorant? I felt so helpless – is his slightly low IQ an explanation for his difficulty to learn school stuff? I tried to tell her that it's difficult to know because there are so many factors. We had been very afraid of how Geoffrey would get on with this year's teacher – the fact that he got on marvellously with her was great. His behavioural difficulties; him hating finding things hard; the teacher he had in the first year of school – who had been horrible. The fact that he has to learn so many things by heart – the fact that he has exams even at a young age (when normally exams start at age 8) (Journal: June, 2005).

I then came across an occupational therapist in my work and learnt about how sometimes difficulties with coordination can interfere with a child's learning in terms of attention, writing, copying from the board, fidgeting in class. I thought about Geoffrey's needs and wondered whether this professional could help him. I hesitated because I thought that he might have had an overload of professionals looking him over. Whenever the mother said that he was coping, I felt better, but, more often than not, the story was that things were getting harder and harder. I finally spoke to the mother about the possibility of referring to an occupational therapist and she said that they would think about it. I pushed a little bit and then backed off totally, thinking that they would let me know if they wanted me to give them her contact number. And yet, I continued to think about it, and to think in ways which were not productive, I thought. I would get all worked up and the insecurity cycle would spring in, starting me thinking about my incompetence again. I felt that I should know the answer, that I was hesitating, that I ought to be able to help this child and that helping him meant giving solutions. What was I doing, just assessing and then not being able to give this family something to work on so that things could improve?

> They see me taking such an interest and they thank me for it – and the interest seems enough – but am I competent in my job? Do they think I'm good because of the interest? If I didn't like the children so much perhaps I might be a better psychologist – more detached – more impartial? Am I reluctant to say something? Even to myself? Am I blinding myself because of my friendship with the family? Is this what professional ethics is about? I thought that because I liked the boy, then that would mean that I would be a better psychologist. Is it possible that there is an optimum level of interest, which I have surpassed to the extent that it is a liability to my work? What about the uncertainty here?
>
> Surely this is a time when certainty is needed. We are going to Nadia, the occupational therapist, to see what she thinks. Maybe she can provide me with some certainty on one aspect of Geoffrey and then we might be able to make our mind up about the other. Is this what I am looking for in Nadia then? Is it because the work of a psychologist is vague and hazy, or is it because I am vague and hazy? (Journal: June, 2005).

This was my constant conundrum. Was it the nature of the work or was it I who was so complex and vague and hard to pin down? I kept veering from one to the other like a pendulum in an attempt to decide. The gladness with which I greeted any clues seemed ridiculous as I thought about the possibility of both being causes of my predicament. While it was certainly possible that I needed to stop undermining myself negatively, it was also the case that a healthy level of self-doubt as a psychologist was a positive thing.

This point came out in one of my conversations with Geoffrey's mother. I was describing to her the uncertainties that I was facing in my studies and work and gave her an example which concerned her son Geoffrey. One way in which his eating might be controlled would be by modifying the family's eating habits. Geoffrey's mother tended to open a packet of biscuits and put them on a plate in the middle of the table, so that everybody could help themselves. Geoffrey inevitably took the largest share of biscuits as it seemed that he ate as though his life depended on it. I contemplated suggesting that Geoffrey's mother would give her children an equal share of the food on separate plates, so that everyone would have his/her due, no more and no less. It would solve the problem of Geoffrey having more than everyone else. However, I hesitated as that would mean that I would be imposing a new value system on the family. I did not want to change the beautiful family dynamic as I thought that Geoffrey and the rest of the family were getting more out of it than simply food. Geoffrey's mother talked about herself as a teacher:

> We were talking about her school and the way in which she feels new ideas are introduced too suddenly. Then she reflected, as though to herself, that no

> one really knows where they're going, that no school really knows the direction it's heading towards. She then turned this onto herself and said that she sometimes feels like that too – or rather always, she added. She said that her husband always tells her that as she's been teaching for so long her preparatory work should be diminishing rather than increasing. As she's been working for such a long time, she should have less work because her resources should be accumulating. And yet, she said, it doesn't feel as though she'd been teaching for so long because there's always so much to worry about.
>
> And I said "But this is probably what makes you a good teacher." I went on to say that that was my experience exactly and was coincidentally what I had been reading about today. The book said that psychiatrists, clinical psychologists, etc. make the mistake of being too sure of themselves, not realising the assumptions, judgements and ideas that they make about people and their work. I told her how I'd been feeling this week – that I was shaky and insecure again and that it's hard because you have to convince people about what you say. You have to appear secure to inspire their trust – and yet ironically they should trust you more because of your insecurity – because it means that you worry more, that you reflect more on what you do. I told her about my difficulties at work because while feeling that my attitude is better in terms of being a reflective practitioner, it sometimes makes me appear a bit woolly and insecure. As yet I find it so hard to express my ideas and argue them with these people who are so confident of their own (Journal: November, 2004).

This needing to appear resolute and convince clients that you are secure of your thoughts and decisions is another factor in the equation. As yet, I have only been mentioning the need to feel secure within the self. The other aspect to it is whether one should communicate one's insecurity to others, especially to the clients in question. Do we owe them this ethically? Or is it enough that they know we are professionals? Perhaps we ought to present to them a convincing face and then trash everything out in supervision. These issues pertaining to professionalism will be discussed in Chapter 8. Here I want to mention that talking these thoughts over with Sylvia had almost a cathartic effect on me as, in the attempt to show her the value of how she worked, I felt the reflection of my words on my own practice. I hastened to write them down in the Journal which is shown above. It was a breakthrough. I felt as though I was being given permission to be uncertain.

Later I was to read about Klein's (1997) distinction between the paranoid-schizoid position and the depressive position and understand it in terms of my own experience as a practitioner. Whenever I started to panic about not knowing and being uncertain what the next step was, I would resist and attempt to delete the experience by looking for things to do and alternatives to try. I apply Klein's splitting process to this situation, in particular her description of the weakening of the ego when undesirable parts of the self are split off and pushed away from the self. This was the way in which I could cope with the frightening realisation that I did not know and that I was being expected to know. It sometimes was the case that the best intervention would be no intervention – and yet I felt unable to admit this and stand by it.

I did not feel that I could argue this to teachers, heads of schools or parents, also because even I was afraid of taking such a stand. A certain amount of this splitting, according to Klein (1997), is however essential and eventually may also lead towards reintegration. Thus, when I allowed myself to not know, to be uncertain, I was then taking Klein's depressive position, in which the ability to accept both good and bad at the same time is possible. "In the depressive position the baby (and later the child and adult) begins to integrate experience rather than to split it. Awareness of objects as a whole, with both loved and hated characteristics, begins. This has considerable consequences. Awareness of the self as a more whole, loving and hating being can also begin. Conflicts between different parts of the self are no longer solved by splitting and pushing those parts into others … but by holding them within the self" (Segal, 2004, p. 41).

The desperate need to have decided ideas in my mind about what it was that I had to do with children started to be balanced with a toleration for the uncertainty which accompanied my practice. This was by no means a state of being which was fixed – I had not reached this point in my development permanently. It was a state of being which sometimes reverted back to the intense fear, until I could understand once more that I could work with children without knowing exactly what to do. What was different was that I now could understand the process, and in so doing, felt less traumatised each time it happened. I was learning about being in a constant state of becoming, tempered with moments of stability, which in their turn served as platforms from which other experiences could be undertaken.

I already referred to Hollway's (1994) idea of the self not necessarily being unified. Through her theory of the non-unitary sense of self, contradictions, uncertainties and insecurities can be acknowledged. People are thus not fixed, but are in constant process, in a state of becoming. Tolerating uncertainty allows one to have this vision of people, and also of oneself. In the next chapter I outline some of Wilfred Bion (1994)'s theories about learning from experience where it relates to this uncertainty in my studies and my work, asking the question whether not knowing the answer with certainty might actually be a positive way of working. The practitioner who can recognise the differences and inconsistencies in dilemmas, in the practitioner's own story and in that of others, is engaged in learning and becoming. Thus an alternative perspective of the practitioner who works with children can be seen.

CHAPTER 6

UNCERTAINTY POSITIVE? A NEW IDEA

1. "MIND PERMEATES OUR BODIES AND VICE VERSA" (BREARLEY, 2002 P. 443)

This chapter introduces Bion's (1994) theories about learning from experience. These theories are then related to the narratives given in previous chapters. Reading Bion can be a struggle, as evidenced in various notes and articles found in journals and on websites, which mention how hard it is to engage with Bion's ideas and equally, how innovative and relevant they are. I was encouraged when I read these as I realised that the concepts which Bion (1994) tried to communicate were still forming in his own mind and it may well be that he struggled to put them down on paper. This is reflected in my own struggle to understand him. In this chapter I explain some of Bion's theories where they are relevant to the previous narratives of research and practice, and also apply them to situations of practice in the helping professions.

The 'model' of mind put forward by Bion suggests that "thinking can be the activity of dealing with, or restricting the effects of incoming stimuli" (Billington, 2000, p. 112). In previous chapters, the difficulty of coping with not being certain is mentioned – I felt pressure to have a decided knowing both from the outside, in the form of expectations of the child's parents and other professionals, and also from within. In the journal which I was keeping, I wrote profusely about sleepless nights in which I worried incessantly about the children with whom I was working at the time. I recall feelings of confusion and fear as it did not seem that I would be able to see a way forward. My mind would be easy prey to all sorts of negative thoughts which were nameless and incoherent. Spinoza (1989) writes about an emotion being a passion when it is a confused idea. "An emotion is bad or harmful only in so far as the mind is prevented by it from thinking" (p. 205). It did not seem that there was any thinking going on as I lay awake in the night, worried and confused. According to Bion (1994), the bewilderment and uncertainty would be symptoms of bodily sensory traces which are the form in which 'undigested facts', more formally known as *beta elements*, are stored. The confusion could be seen as facts, perceptions, or impressions which are as yet undigested. As impressions of the senses and of affection which are as yet raw, the psychic and physical are indistinguishable. The amount of time spent staring into nothing (as I ponder over something without knowing it) and the amount of sleepless hours are the outward effects of undigested facts on myself. Bion's ideas will be expanded further on in this chapter. Brearley (2002) says that 'it is our job to reflect' and writes about his experience in his paper on the body-mind problem:

> Feeling anxious about the task of writing this paper, and of having formed something interesting to say to you, I can't sleep. Half-formed thoughts career

> around my mind. In retrospect, I might describe my state as a mixture of fear and excitement. In the middle of the night I feel more than usually perplexed about body and mind questions, and the hopelessness of any possible solution (p. 437).

If I were to describe my own state of being in such a time, I would have to focus on the short breaths that I take and the consciousness of my mind going like a broken record. There is intense physical discomfort and fatigue, but still sleep eludes me as my eyes are wide open in some kind of anticipation, or should I say, apprehension. I feel as bad physically as I would be feeling mentally although they do not seem to be at all related. Everything seems to be caught in some kind of vicious circle, a trap from which there is no way out. In vain I try to take deep breaths in order to calm myself down, and also attempt to visualise a calm, relaxed environment in the hope of overcoming what seems to be a state of anxiety and panic. Both body and mind seem stuck. Spinoza calls these "emotions which are contrary to our nature" and says that they "are bad in so far as they prevent the mind from understanding" (1989, p. 206).

> In the middle of this confusion, I get cramp in my calves and feet. I have to jump out of bed, and arch and press my feet to the ground. Here I am, with a somatic symptom of the very process that I am intellectually stuck in, the kind of intellectual cramp Wittgenstein refers to. The wretched body won't stay out of the picture (Brearley, 2002, p. 437).

Bion's (1994) work emphasises the connection between emotion, which comes from experience, and learning. These often isolated aspects of human functioning are married together as inseparable. According to Bion (1994), emotion and cognition are very much related, to such an extent that unless both work together, learning cannot take place. The very integration of thoughts comes about following a very important process in which both conscious and unconscious impressions are rendered accessible to the personality. Damasio (1999) calls this consciousness, which "is the rite of passage which allows an organism … to become a minded organism.… Spinoza said that the effort to preserve oneself is the first and unique foundation of virtue. Consciousness enables that effort" (p. 25). Without this process described by Bion (1994), not only can the person not formulate and put meaning to ideas, but also cannot use such thoughts for other functions such as memory. Thus, this function in the psyche operates to transform sense impressions of all kinds from raw, undigested material into material which can be used (Segal, 2004, p. 125). "To facilitate thinking about this unknown process which he believed had some resemblance to dreaming, Bion labelled it *alpha function* and the products of its action he termed *alpha elements*.… By naming it alpha function, Bion hoped to be able to keep the concept open to avoid the premature imposition of meaning" (Symington and Symington, 1996, p. 61).

> In summary, beta and alpha elements are hypothetical entities for which there may be no realization, but they are convenient for talking about something which is in the sensuous realm and therefore not human thought (beta elements), and something that is becoming a thought (alpha elements) (ibid., p. 71).

2. NOT STICKING TO 'FACTS'

Why is the state of confusion so frightening? As already explained in previous chapters, as educational psychologists, we are perceived to deal in facts. Psychologists, as well as other caring professionals, are increasingly called upon "to provide precise, absolute knowledge about children" (Billington, 2000, p. 98). There is an illusion that aspects of people can be compartmentalised. A child either has dyslexia, or s/he does not; a child either has attention deficit disorder or s/he does not. However, it seems as though it is never the case for me. Somehow, none of the cases in which I get involved seem to be so clear cut. The question needs to be asked: do I coincidentally get the cases which are difficult to diagnose? or am I not sharp enough to notice signs and symptoms and thus hesitate to diagnose? All the professionals around me seem to be so sure of what they are doing and I seem to flounder about ineffectively, and also inefficiently. It may look as though I ought to be permanently closing more cases than I actually do. Moreover, when a case is actually closed and filed, I consistently do not fill the empty space on the cover of the file in which the disorder/condition/cause of child's difficulty should be written. Sometimes I am expected to do so for the sake of keeping a record and I hesitate to put down something too definite. Instead I write down something vague like "emotional difficulties" or "social difficulties" or "learning difficulties". Giving a child a label for the sake of record-keeping is the wrong reason, I believe, also because I am often tempted to say that the primary cause of the difficulties that a child presents with stems from the child's environment. However, this is not present in the list of possible labels which can be written on the cover of the file. How many times do we want to write on the cover of the file 'teacher with burn-out' or 'parents who abuse drugs' or even 'unkind adult being blatantly cruel to a child who is not going to sit back and take it'.

Thus, the question which we perhaps ought to be asking is whether cases are ever really as clear cut as we were led to think. Perhaps the work of educational psychologists is not to see the facts and decide on the diagnosis (couldn't a computer programme do that in the same way as it analyses the data for the researcher?) It is very difficult to give a diagnosis of attention deficit disorder to a ten year old boy if the boy's visual perceptual difficulties require such a great effort from him that he gets tired and loses concentration earlier than other 'normal' children. The boy's behaviour is the same as that stated in the Diagnostic and Statistical Manual IV under the subheading Attention Deficit Disorder. However, I hesitate to give this boy such a label, considering all the other information.

In another case, I am required to write a report so that classroom support can be applied for, because this boy is constantly playing up and being aggressive in class. The boy presents as a classic Attention Deficit/Hyperactivity Disorder of the Oppositional type. Yet, knowing the constant instability that this boy experiences at home, am I justified in applying the AD/HD label? Another fourteen year old boy was referred to me. He is very frustrated because of a myriad of related factors: he is adopted and is in a phase where he is feeling it, he is fourteen, and he is fed up of trying his hardest to overcome his specific learning difficulties and organisation difficulties with no concrete results. He is being very rude and constantly plays up at school. The head teacher asked me, hopefully, whether we could call Arthur a boy with Oppositional Defiance Disorder (ODD), as his behaviour resembled that of another child in the same school with such a diagnosis. I tactfully said that although the behaviour was the same, the cause was different. I refrained from implying that I doubted whether this other boy with the ODD diagnosis actually had ODD anyway.

Every case seems to me to be made up of a complex interrelation of factors which accumulate and leave their own effects on the situation which the child is in. Nothing seems clear cut, and sometimes, some things seem more confusing than others. It is not only psychotherapists or clinical psychologists who should doubt themselves and their movement with a client. Educational psychologists, social workers, teachers and other helping professionals should do so too – we ought not to feel complacent with our knowledge of *facts* – facts, without the child's and family's story behind them, do not stand. They must be seen in the complicated context which is people's lives. In our involvement with our clients, we should consider ourselves as having relationships which are prey to those kinds of dynamics which we accept that the therapist-client relationship has. Thus I believe that the following statement made by Brearley (2002) on the dynamics of analysis is also relevant to us as caring professionals. If it is not, then perhaps it ought to be.

> One counter-transference problem that such [clients] tend to evoke in us is the need to think we know; we may then be tempted to be wild analysts, constructing, and offering, heroic, magical and omniscient interpretations (p. 430). (my own substitution of the word 'patients' with 'clients').

Thus it is essential that as professionals we wonder whether we are doing the right thing when we discount what the mother is saying because we know better. How can one be sure that we know better? Perhaps a parent's seemingly overly-protective and controlling manner is a *consequence* of her difficulties and not the *cause* of them. Questions like this and the above on specific cases in which I am involved are typical causes of my lack of sleep at night and rumination during the day.

> What I hope to do in this paper is consider some of the anxiety that I can feel in this area of my work (Brearley, 2002, p. 431).

3. BION AND 'FACTS'

Rather than aiding and abetting us to pin ourselves down and be certain of ourselves and the world around us, Bion "bursts open the possibility of understanding what lies beyond the trajectories of our current abilities to think" (Horne *et al.*, 2000, p. 115). He believes that it is "un-psychoanalytical to adhere to some rigid system as a substitute for using our minds" (Bion, 1990, p. 201, in ibid.) In the same way, I argue that it is against what we ought to be doing as helping professionals to stick to rigid facts and be blind to the medley of influences and factors which reality is made up of. "Achievement … [is] capable of being in uncertainties, mysteries, doubts without any irritable reaching after fact and reason" (Keats in Bion 1970, p. 125). So it is possible to speculate without seeming incompetent or lacking knowledge (Billington, 2000, p. 98). Having strict notions of causality is one way of being rigid and Bion rather speaks of suspension of ideas and "particularly, the suspension of memory and desire which may be attached to determinism and teleology. Possibly Bion considered causality a dogmatism which evaded the immediacy and complexity of experience, thus stripping it of aesthetic qualities and denuding meaning itself" (Horne *et al.*, 2000, p. 115).

Indeed, Bion could be considered as a post-structuralist, in philosophical terms, as he seems to reject the modern notions of reason and science as tools which give us the why and wherefore of things. Indeed, Sandler (1997) quotes Bion stressing on many occasions the fact that some problems faced by psychoanalysts always faced philosophers of science (p. 50). Bion himself did try to create a model of the mind (The Grid in Bion, 1994); he did try to etch the ways in which he believed the mind worked in stone (Symington and Symington, 1996). This attempt, though, was good enough for Bion to realise its inadequacy.

Bion agrees with deconstructionists that a diagnosis says more about the person giving the diagnosis than about the person it is given to. "The use of medical terminology also affects those who are responsible for labelling" (Parker *et al.*, 1995, p. 2). "Issues of causality…relate more to 'the peace of mind of the discoverer than to the object of his research' (Bion 1967, p. 163)" (Horne *et al.*, 2000, p. 115). What is significant for Bion is how selected facts are linked together in one's psyche, how the slightest awareness of what is unknowable puts a heavy strain on it, and the importance of the effort of tolerating elements and links. He believes that in moments of crises the anxieties which are generated mean that "we are not the creators of our thoughts but that thoughts are pressed on us" (Horne *et al.*, 2000, p. 117). In fact he is quoted to say "Thinking has to be called into existence to cope with thought" (Bion, 1994, p. 111).

How do we find meaning in experience? Material for thinking and dreaming is made up of *alpha elements* which are developed by the *alpha function*. Bion (1994) used this name as he wanted to describe 'an essence in process'. The essence comes together through the tension of us holding separate bits through links. What links thought is alive and provides us with insight and meaning. Thus, when an emotional experience is transformed into alpha elements, dream-thoughts are formed to make unconscious waking thinking and also to make storage in the mind possible. Only through this process of thinking can we tolerate the thought which is thrust upon us.

> Alpha function acts on the data from a person's total emotional experience, which includes those arising out of the sensory input from external and internal sources. It renders this emotional experience comprehensible and meaningful, by producing alpha elements consisting of visual, auditory and olfactory impressions, which are storable in memory, usable in dreaming and in unconscious waking thinking. The latter includes the input into thinking of images stored in memory which add richness to the conscious thought content (Symington and Symington, 1997, p. 61).

However, thoughts are not always welcome in our mind. We may not be ready for the experience which is thrust upon us. To continue with the food analogy adopted by Bion (1994), we may have eaten enough for the day and have full stomachs, or some stressful experience may have happened to put us off food and we find digestion difficult. Thus transformation by the alpha function into alpha elements may not be immediately possible and the events which cannot be entertained in the mind are called *beta elements*, 'facts' which are still 'undigested'. "They are sense impressions devoid of meaning or nameless sensations which cause frustration" (Symington and Symington, 1997, p. 62). When something is a sore point with a person then that is a sign of an 'undigested fact' which has not been converted into alpha elements to be available for processing and storage. That person's dealing with such a sore point is indicative of what we know as unfinished business and we can all identify with the discomfort felt. Beta elements are not in a condition which can be put into words – "once we have put words to them they are no longer beta elements, but alpha elements" (Segal, 2004, p. 125).

I am aware of the experience, when doing casework, of trying to take in all the information that is being directly and also nonverbally given in my meetings with people. I am conscious of some of the judgements that I form there and then. However, other impressions are taken in unnoticed and unawares. They trouble me later, when it should be time for me to rest. Bion's (1994) word 'undigested' is very apt, as I am kept awake, as though I had just eaten some food and have trouble digesting it. And, although I cannot physically rest, still the undigested facts do not surface. They are there, like an irritating itch which I cannot pinpoint. These 'raw' impressions, these beta elements, are not yet ready for me to think about – I cannot yet tolerate the sensations which accompany these impressions.

A distinction needs to be made between memories and 'undigested facts', as the former are available for thought and are the result of alpha function processing. Undigested facts, beta elements, have yet to go through this process and become memories. My undigested facts in the story of my involvement with Geoffrey took the form of anxiety, worry, a wish to avoid the subject. It was because I was not yet able to tolerate the idea that I did not know with certainty. I believed that I was almost omniscient, that I ought to know. It was further validated by colleagues who implied that I did not know only because I was inexperienced.

> Often we will not know what to believe. But however uncertain we are, we have our psychoanalytic experience and understanding to help us to be open to the patient's vibes or projections. We have an idea of what sorts of material would count as evidence, and we know that further evidence, including the patient's responses, may lead us to withdraw, revise, qualify, confirm or expand our earlier ideas. Naturally, we often don't know; but we have an idea of what it would be to know more (Brearley, 2002, p. 431).

What do I worry about? Very often, there would be a child with whom I would be working and I would worry about the 'what ifs' and 'hows' as I think that I must come up with something to help this child, what to come up with and the ramifications of such ideas. Other, more side issues, also come into the picture as I feel that I am going to lose face. But it all boils down to the fear that I might be doing something wrong and that I do not know much. I cannot tolerate being uncertain,

I cannot tolerate the risks that I am taking with people's lives. I believe that this is because of the fear which is often felt that I might not be able to help the people encountered in the casework. It seems as though it takes me time to learn to live with such fear – to understand that it stems from some impulse which is brave, rather than cowardly. One needs to be brave when one is aware of how fragile some people are when they approach a psychologist. One needs to be brave to be cautious and respectful of their humanity and individuality. One needs to be brave in order to be conscious of the risks that are involved in working with people who put their faith in one's 'expertise'.

When I spoke to a colleague about uncertainty, and expressed my thoughts that uncertainty could be embraced, his reply was that I will find, with the passing of time, that my uncertainty will diminish. Somehow we were not speaking on the same wavelength – he could not conceive the positivity of being uncertain – he may have forgotten its uses when he started embracing certainty. Incredibly, some practitioners in the helping professions do not seem to have the space to be therapeutic with themselves – if there were this space, then these issues would be normal everyday things. There is a great need for such a space and time as it could be quite dangerous for educational psychologists, social workers, counsellors, etc. to continue thinking that they ought to know it all, and that they in fact do know most of it at least.

Not yet realising this, I yearned for that certainty and totally blocked my ability to think because of the insecurity I felt for what I believed was lack of sufficient knowledge. My inward reaction when the paediatrician in the story of Geoffrey in Chapter 5 supposed the same syndrome which I had suspected was one of total triumph that I had "got it" and also of chagrin that I had "chickened out" of saying it. I wanted to feel responsible for it. In fact, I actually told the mother that it was what I had in my mind all along. This was true but my reason for saying it was totally self-motivated.

Bion's (1994) beta elements are not genuine memories, they are unavailable for thought – they thus need to be selected and interpreted so that they can be recycled as genuine memories (thus they can be forgotten or recalled). This could be seen as a kind of retranscription as, through learning from an emotional experience, "the mind builds itself, bit by bit, by digesting experiences" (Meltzer, 1984, p. 42 in Da Silva, 1997). This is the way in which emotional development takes place (Andrade de Azevedo, 2000, p. 84). When digestion, or metabolisation, does not take place, these facts remain "the unrememberable and the unforgettable" (Alvin Frank, 1969 in Guy Da Silva, 1997). According to Bion (1994), this is owing to the lack of the 'contact barrier' which separates the conscious from the unconscious, which contact barrier is developed by the alpha function. "Its permeability allows some interchange between the two but not a swamping of one by the other ... It is while this membrane is being produced that there is an ongoing correlation of conscious and unconscious elements which, after abstraction, results in comprehension of the emotional experience. It also allows for storage in memory and for repression" (Symington and Symington, 1997, p. 65). If this contact barrier is not set up, sense-impressions continue untransformed to burden and trouble the mind and it is not possible to think about them consciously. Andrade de Azevedo (2000) mentions borderline and psychotic patients as examples of persons who do not develop the notion of consciousness as being the organ for sensorially apprehending psychic qualities.

The question is what is envisaged as a result of the changing from beta elements to alpha elements by the alpha function. Am I arguing that the uncertainty which is resisted when in the form of beta elements be changed to certainty through alpha function? This would be to fall in the same trap of binary positions of certainty and uncertainty, with a hankering after knowing of facts that will change the uncertainty into certainty. My argument (which will be further developed later in the chapter) is that certainty does not imply knowledge of facts, and therefore uncertainty is not a lack of knowledge of facts. The position which one is in when beta elements do not allow for digestion means that one is resisting being uncertain. The transformation of those beta elements into alpha elements means that one becomes able to live with uncertainty, to take this position as the attitude which will best serve the clients with whom one works. Thus the choice is not between uncertainty and certainty, but it is living with uncertainty.

This ties in with the arguments that were put forward in earlier chapters, that this process is what contributes to further becoming. It brings to mind Klein's (1997) depressive position, when both the good and bad can be viewed within the same object without threat to the person. Living with uncertainty without being frightened requires a shift in perspective, where uncertainty is not a position which is to be rejected as bad, but a state of being which contributes to growth and becoming. It is a state of being which one wants to reach.

When I consciously give attention to what troubles me, I feel as though I am bringing these subtle impressions to the surface, that my hitherto ignored intuitions are heard. As Spinoza writes "An emotion which is a passion ceases to be a passion as soon as we form a clear and distinct idea of it" (1989, p. 202), having said, as quoted above, that a passion is a confused idea and prevents the mind from understanding. "Therefore the more an emotion becomes known to us, the more it is within our power and the less the mind is passive in regard to it" (Spinoza, 1989, p. 202). When I am able to tolerate the sensations and frustration which accompany the incoming stimuli (Billington, 2000, p. 2), I become conscious of my emotional experience and am able to abstract from it a statement that will represent this experience adequately. In this way, these impressions and intuitions are available for thought. Joanna Field (1990) adequately expresses thoughts prior to conscious thought as *blind*: "…whenever my thought was 'blind', that is, whenever I was not aware of what I was thinking, then my thoughts were liable to be quite childish and unreasonable" (p. 15).

Damasio (1999) makes a distinction between 'feeling' and 'knowing that we have a feeling', emphasising that consciousness must be present if feelings are to influence beyond the here and now. In fact, he claims that consciousness is "the key to a life examined, for better and for worse.… At its simplest and most basic level, consciousness lets us recognise an irresistible urge to stay alive and develop a concern for the self. At its most complex and elaborate level, consciousness helps us develop a concern for other selves and improve the art of life" (p. 5). Damasio also suggests that the result of neuropsychological studies indicate that a lack of emotion is as prejudicial for rationality as excessive emotion (Spinoza's passion). "It certainly does not seem true that reason stands to gain from operating without the leverage of emotion. On the contrary, emotion probably assists reasoning…" (p. 41).

Through becoming conscious of the emotional experience, I become able to work with it. I apply Bion's (1994) ideas both to my research and also to my work with children. Besides the fact that my research work is based on my work with children, and on reflecting how I approach this kind of work, I also argue that this research went through a similar process of thought. As mentioned in Chapter 4 my previous research experiences took the form of me feeling as though I was procrastinating because I did not know what I wanted to focus my study on, and eventually skipping the circumspection phase in order to 'get started'. I used to envy my friends in their knowledge of who they were and what they wanted to do. I tried to imitate them with results which left much to be desired.

4. APPLYING THIS TO RESEARCH AND PRACTICE?

In Chapter 4 a therapeutic point was introduced, when immediacy was seen as what managed to bring what was underlying into the here and now and to extend its effects beyond the present in a way that was beneficial to the therapeutic process. This links with the conversion of beta elements into alpha elements by the alpha function. In fact, as Segal explains:

> A counsellor or therapist can sometimes take in frightening sense elements from the client and enable the client to convert them into thoughts and words. 'I've never spoken of this before' is a sign that a particular kind of symbolisation is taking place for the first time. Feelings which were previously only available to be evoked in someone else may be named; this is why it is important for counsellors and therapists to learn to put words to 'what is happening between us' because it is in this relationship that the nameless beta elements are active (2004, p. 125).

One of my aims in this research is to see whether being uncertain in practice could also be positive. There has been a transition from a constant sense of feeling that not enough is known, to an acknowledgement that it is important that although one does know, one can still be uncertain. This does not imply a life of constant uncertainty and instability, but an acceptance of those moments when uncertainty prevails as opposed to a resistance of those moments. Of course it is positive that one continues to study and learn, but this is not a move towards certainty.

I do not find being an educational psychologist easy. There is not an amount of knowledge which I need to know, after which I can feel that I am an expert and that what I say goes. That would be easy. I was always good at studying facts – I remember and reproduce them more or less correctly. But having this kind of knowledge might not be what it takes to be an educational psychologist, or perhaps to be a good educational psychologist. Colleagues amaze me with the amount of knowledge that they have. When faced with such knowledge, I always felt ignorant and unworthy and I retreated from the discussion. I told myself over and over that I should know more. I started to think that I was weak because my will did not push enough to make me wake up early and to read as much. "I had assumed that there was something in me called will which only had to command in order to be obeyed" (Field, 1990, p. 97).

> For a long time I was continually putting off the next step in my exploration because I felt I ought to know more, knew there were many books written about these things, felt that I must read them all before I could go any further. Whenever I gave in to this impulse I found it disastrous (Field, 1990, p. 33).

Yet at the same time, I tried to reason with myself that I could probably continue reading forever and still feel inadequate. I had to rate how much of this feeling of inadequacy was caused by a real lack of knowledge, and how much was caused by the lack of tolerance for not knowing.

> It took me years to learn that I must never begin my search by looking in books, never say, 'I know too little, I must read some more before I start', but that I must always observe first, express what I observed, and then, if I needed it, see what the books had to say … I had tried to read a good deal of literature…it had always completely dampened my enthusiasm for discovery, leaving me in despair with a burden of guilt because there was so much I did not understand (ibid., p. 33).

Reading is always a good idea. But perhaps what I really needed to do was to appreciate my self and my attitude towards being an educational psychologist. "…instead of trying to force myself into doing what I imagined I ought to do I began to enquire into what I was doing" (Field, 1990, p. 25). Billington (2000) criticises the training and practices of professionals, which, he says, "are based upon thinking which is stripped of its vitality and organised in beta-elements, and are thus characterised by the accretion of 'pieces' of dead knowledge" (p. 113). Perhaps this was what was positive – the certainty that I would be confused about each case would ensure my taking each case individually and see it as made up of a multitude of factors which made it unique. However, I found that my practice was taking over the rest of my life, in that, I would worry constantly and be miserable about it. I wished I could be self-assured as I perceived others were. Yet, according to Billington (2000), "these pieces of knowledge merely substitute for a more active thinking and learning which, by comparison, are characterised by movement and relations-to, which are able to tolerate stimuli and which, crucially, are able to tolerate the uncertainty of not knowing" (Billington, 2000, p. 113).

For the purposes of my research, I discovered that feeling lost was part of the process. It may be that I have been taking in pieces of knowledge and pieces of experience, which pieces were seen as disparate and unconnected, whereas now that I can let myself process them, and can and have tolerated the frustration and anxiety, they are slowly taking shape. Links are being formed. I seem to have resigned myself to feeling unsure – to realise that perhaps feeling unsure is the best way towards good practice.

> This complex process results in the possibility of the evolution of the mind that will be able to develop thoughts. From this point of view, the capacity to

> dream is what safeguards the personality from a psychotic state, where no contact barrier is formed by alpha elements, nor is there a distinction between consciousness and unconsciousness (Andrade de Azevedo, 2000, p. 85).

Thus, from resignation, my perspective is shifting to accommodation, as I see the need to stop my want for certainty and to work with the moments of uncertainty which occur when working with children. So the confusion which I experience and which caused me a lot of concern, is what I have to, not only resign myself to, but befriend and use to my advantage. This is what happens when beta elements change to alpha elements, so that thoughts develop and growth takes place. In this way, I can abstract a workable statement for my research work, which indicated that the big ideas which my supervisor described in my writing concern the dilemmas in professional practice. I have since striven to be able to research systematically and write about them.

In my practice I have been teaching myself to shift my focus away from longing for certainty and towards an acknowledgement that I cannot continue to look towards that day when I will have become a professional educational psychologist who *knows*. Today, everyday, I am in a constant state of becoming an educational psychologist already because I acknowledge that there is no simple answer to difficulties, that each case merits its own time and mental space and that I need not fear not knowing. The practitioner is in a constant state of becoming, with every action that is taken in practice. Chapter 11 expands further on this note and mentions *phronesis*, which is what aids judgement of what is to be done in day to day practice.

Thus, in the same way as I started to realise that being confused was probably a good thing for my research, it was likewise a good thing for my practice as an educational psychologist. My job was, not to read more, or not only to read more, but also to start appreciating my uncertainty and ignorance. The willingness to suspend judgment, the willingness not to allow oneself to know, made space for a new kind of understanding (Hinshelwood, 1998, p. 118). In the same way that Billington sees pieces of dead knowledge as beta-elements, the ruminations and worrying, and sleepless hours could also be symptoms of the 'undigested facts' where the psychic and the physical are indistinguishable. The intolerance of uncertainty and frustration made these facts unavailable for thought and, as such, they could not become memories. In fact, as previously mentioned, Joanna Field (1990) calls such facts childish and unreasonable thoughts, and indeed, upon reflection, my behaviour when I worry is rather childish, and reminds me of when I used to lie awake in bed as a child, terrified of some unknown monster that my imagination would evoke.

Learning to live with this consciousness, which may be a better word to use rather than fear, means that the emotional experiences and impressions need to be transformed into alpha elements. Thus, I can abstract from the consciousness of this emotional experience a statement which I can function with, a statement which represents this experience. This is when I started to think about dilemmas being the centre of my work, both in terms of research as well as my professional practice. These dilemmas are very often taken for granted – however, the very fact that the spotlight is thrown on them, that they are pronounced, already starts serving the purpose of practice, or research. By pronouncing what is obvious, one can then problematise that pronunciation and it becomes something which can be worked with, whether this means tolerated or changed. In Joanna Field's (1990) words, "writing down my experiences … seemed to be a creative act which continually lit up new possibilities in what I had seen" (Field, 1990, p. 44).

CONCLUSION

This chapter has focused more on the self and on how the formation of the practitioner and of the researcher is influenced by different processes. The next chapter is a natural progression of this, in that, the focus is more on the practice of the practitioner in terms of the role and how it affects others. It was important to establish the possibility and positivity of having uncertainty in the work of the expert professional thus far. The next chapters extend these ideas to include the interaction of the professional with others.

> The essence of core consciousness is the very thought of you – the very feeling of you – as an individual being involved in the process of knowing of your own existence and of the existence of others (Damasio, 1999, p. 127).

CHAPTER 7

THE PERSONAL AND THE PROFESSIONAL

This chapter and the next explore the dilemmas around the professional role of the helping practitioner in education which is the second theme of this book. Using educational psychologists as a starting point, the question what is it that caring professionals do is asked. This is expanded to the question how one can see the effects of the work of the educational psychologist and other caring professionals, and furthermore how to evaluate such work, since the discussion indicates that there is not one standard way of noting success. The argument is taken that the common factor in many views on the practitioners' role is that the child's welfare is of primary concern. Some of the dilemmas of fulfilling such a role are explored. Namely, the question of the personal and professional is put forward, the question being what kind of good practice is possible, if the practitioner's aim is to be solely professional and to leave his/her personal self aside. Considering that the work of the helping professional in education is to deal with the personal lives of people, namely vulnerable children, there may be a contradiction in the thought that the professional life of the practitioner can interact with the personal life of the child.

I argue that it might be beneficial if the personal life of the practitioner were to be kept less firmly away from the professional life. This means that the practitioner can understand and empathise with the people that she works with better because she can draw upon her own experiences. It also implies that the practitioner is in tune with her own reactions and emotions which may be evoked by the situations which are presented. Sometimes a helping professional can be more helpful to the person with whom she is involved if she can put herself into that person's shoes. It thus becomes harder to see the people whom one should be helping as numbers on a list. It is as though a professional interest in a child's well-being may not be enough as other claims on a practitioner's time may make it hard for that practitioner to give the attention she may believe that a child/ parent/ teacher needs. I believe that a more personal interest would be a better guarantee of the kind of attitude and stance which is helpful for persons that the practitioner is involved with.

1. WHAT IS THE WORK OF AN EDUCATIONAL PSYCHOLOGIST?

> Colleagues of EPNET,
>
> What is our basic work? If there was just one thing?
>
> Is there one sentence you might use to sum up what educational psychologists do?
>
> (Educational Psychologist, no.1 EPNET 24 August 2005)

> How about – 'EPs make psychological sense of people's concerns about children's educational difficulties in ways that facilitate positive change'.
>
> (Educational Psychologist, no.2 EPNET 24 August 2005)
>
> I liked your question so here is my 'script', which I adapt as appropriate, depending on who is asking the question....
>
> 'The EP input can be viewed as an applied psychology facility through which any concern, whether at individual, group, and/ or whole organisation level can be researched in order to locate ways of effecting better understanding and positive change'.
>
> (Educational Psychologist, no.3 EPNET 25 August 2005)
>
> Educational psychology consists of the application of psychological principles in the context of all settings which affect a child's welfare and education.
>
> (Educational Psychologist, no.4 EPNET 25 August 2005)
>
> Educational Psychologists address so as to improve the learning and behaviour of clients utilising core skills obtained in their teaching and psychology training also experiential knowledge gained through professional practice.
>
> (Educational Psychologist, no.5 EPNET 25 August 2005)
>
> Would anyone go with this sentence?
>
> The educational psychologist works with schools and others to support the inclusion of as many children and young people into their local community mainstream school. This may involve using a range of skills, from individual assessment to supporting and challenging schools and the LEA.
>
> (Educational Psychologist, no.1 EPNET 25 August 2005)

As can be seen from the dates beneath each contribution, this debate on EPNET, an email service for educational psychologists, took place in the summer of 2005, and did not come to a definite conclusion, at least, not one which satisfies all the stakeholders who are educational psychologists and those who come into contact with them. The entries which I have quoted above are the first few, following which several discussions emerged about the language used and concepts addressed. It is interesting that whereas in an educational psychologist's job description accompanying an advertisement for a vacancy, the roles involved in that *particular* job are outlined, still it is hard to pinpoint without causing debate what the work of an educational psychologist involves.

Norwich (2005) quotes a "Government report on educational psychology services" which says that the role of the psychologist is "'to promote child development and learning through the application of psychology by working with individuals and groups of children, teachers, and other adults in schools, families, other LEA officers, health and social service and other agencies' (DfEE, 2000)". Still Norwich asks "whether one needs to be a professional psychologist to use psychological knowledge and understanding?" (2005, p. 2). He actually questions whether it might not be a more efficient use of resources to train teachers and assistants in psychology, because these professions use psychology anyway: "Psychology is everywhere, even if it is the kind of psychology that academically trained psychologists might question. Often the psychology is hidden from those using it; it is built into the practices and materials used by teachers, teaching assistants and allied professionals" (ibid., p. 7). This is an interesting point which I would like to explore – psychology is not a software package which can be 'used' by different professionals. By no means am I implying that psychology is meant only for an elite group. However, as I expand further in Chapter 11, psychologists go through a certain formation, such as teachers have their own formation, social workers, and so on.

Educational psychologists are held by different people in different regard. On the one hand, there are those who hold grudges against educational psychologists because of the labelling that they are perceived to stand for. Other people see psychologists as the answer to a prayer and, as mentioned in the previous chapters addressing uncertainty, as people who *know* what to do in a problematic situation. Others still see psychologists as helping to bring about change, but in such a way as to have the persons involved in a situation believe that the change came from them and not from an outside expert.

Furthermore, there are different views as to whether a psychologist works with a problematic child, or whether the situation is seen as problematic. As McNab (2001) says, the different actors and institutions involved in a child's education have different constructions and experiences of a difficult situation. "Schools (and others) construe the problems that teachers experience in terms of the characteristics of children, and perceive them as the child's 'problems' or 'difficulties'. This can mislead us into thinking that the place to seek solutions is in a detailed delineation of the child's qualities and characteristics" (McNab, 2001, point 8). As will be seen in the story of Gemma recounted later in this chapter, it is easier for the adults, including professionals, to locate the problem within the child, however unjust this may seem. Otherwise there would be some very threatening situations in which a professional might have to try and convince a child's parents that they are greatly contributing to the issue, or even a child's teacher. A child cannot really defend herself – it may be safer for the status quo if the child is seen as problematic, rather than to focus on how all the actors in a situation contribute to it (including the educational psychologist). It is important to keep in mind that adults ask for the intervention of an educational psychologist when *they* have a problem interacting with a child, whether this is in the form of teaching, managing behaviour, or fostering the child's development. The child never refers herself. "The characteristics of the child are famously secondary: teachers in one school or class may have problems in educating children with exactly similar characteristics to those who are unproblematic in another school or class." (McNab, 2001, point 9).

This then leads to the debate on who is the receiver of the service provided by the educational psychologist.

> In the case of a request for collaborative work, there may be considerable murkiness in the minds of the various participants (including the EP!) about who is, or should be, in the relationship of Customer, Recipient, and Beneficiary

> to the process. Teachers may be surprised to discover that they themselves are in a Recipient or Beneficiary relationship; and parents, too, may stand in these relationships to the process.... This situation can give rise to awkwardness or conflict: the adults may only be prepared to think of themselves as being in the Customer relationship to the EP's work (McNab, 2005, points 8–9).

This variety of views is by no means comprehensive and is further complicated by the fact that the above views are not only held by *others* but also by educational psychologists themselves. This group of professionals cannot be said to have a common voice on what constitutes their work. I do not believe that educational psychologists are alone in this respect – in fact, many members of different professions would profess the same. Some educational psychologists have attempted to put their thoughts down on paper on how they perceive the nature of their work:

> It should now be clear why the seemingly simple question 'who is the client?' is in fact inherently problematic: it conflates important distinctions about the role relationship people have to a particular piece of work.... Clarity about these distinctions matters, especially when one comes to consider whom one would approach for "client feedback" or to seek the "customer's views" about the quality of a piece of work. Distinguishing who are the Customers, Recipients, Beneficiaries, Partners, and Stakeholders in relation to a particular job is important to the reliability and validity of quality assurance and quality management.... For example (and fairly obviously), Customers and Recipients may not have the same view about a piece of work. The Customer may not have consulted the Recipient; or the Recipient may have very different goals from those of the Customer. Indeed, the person seen as the Recipient or Beneficiary by the Customer may not themselves feel that they require the job the Customer wants at all! (McNab, 2005, points 22–24).

> Even when there is manifest success, the observable outcomes are a complex result of the activities of many people, and the connections between the outcomes and the work of the EP cannot easily be disentangled. Indeed, it is arguable that consultation has been most successful when the contribution of the EP is least obvious, since the psychology of the process is about empowering people to create their own solution. There should be no residue of the catalyst in the products of a well-designed chemical reaction (McNab, 2001, point 4).

> "I have also argued that if we recognise the dilemmas in sustaining a profession of applied psychology, we would be aware of our precarious roles, while still believing in the critical importance of psychology for human well-being. The essential task is for professional psychologists to be innovative in service terms, to ensure a continuing and valued position in this network, with one eye on theoretical-linked and evidence-informed developments, and the other on trends in policy, service and inter-professional work. This is the challenge" (Norwich, 2005, p. 9).

If even psychologists are questioning their role, whether this is which technique or approach to adopt, or even questioning the necessity of that role, how then can *others* know what to expect when an educational psychologist is called on a scene?

2. MY APPROACH TO THE WORK OF AN EDUCATIONAL PSYCHOLOGIST

In previous chapter I gave some examples of incidents which indicated to me that educational psychologists were not very well regarded by some other professionals. Why is this so? We work with children in order to *help* them, not to harm them. If, following the intervention of a psychologist, a child is worse off than she was prior to the intervention, then that intervention cannot have been a positive one, and something must have gone wrong somewhere. Even if the outcome of a psychologist's intervention is just to maintain the status quo, it can be the case that maintenance of the current state of being is more desirable at least than worse circumstances. "...preventing things from getting worse can be as important as making things better ... And keeping things going with fewer resources, with less 'exclusion' or segregation, may be the best that can be achieved and may count as success where otherwise there might have been utter failure" (McNab, 2001). The work of a psychologist is sometimes quite difficult to see as it involves negotiation around the mind-sets of the actors in a situation. Although the children are the ones being referred, the 'problem situation' involves everybody who has come in contact with that child.

There is, however, another side to the story. I have confidence that educational psychologists' involvement with individual children is as explained above. Perhaps the negative side to our profession is how we deal with those other children whom we have not yet met. When referrals come before us, they are faceless, and it is easier to be firmer and more assertive with boundaries. One may feel the pressures of too much work as one sees the pile of referral forms increase and the reaction may be to resist. On an individual basis the practitioner may feel impelled to participate, to become involved, whereas while the child is still a name, a number, without a face, the matter is different. How then is one to evaluate the work of educational psychologists? Can one "count the number of children who 'got better' – the number whose reading scores went up, or whose misbehaviour decreased"? (McNab, 2001). This would be, as McNab says, quite a simple-minded evaluation. The outcomes of the intervention of a psychologist are often more subtle: sometimes problems cannot be solved but "teachers [may] find better ways to cope: the child remains included in the ordinary class, other children do not suffer, and the teacher feels more skilled and less stressed" (McNab, 2001). How does one measure a situation which was contained and prevented from getting worse? Would that be deemed a success, or simply maintaining the status quo?

The quotations from the emails with which this chapter started seem to have as their common factor the aim of the child's well-being. I want to stress that the educational psychologist's work is to try to bring about that situation which is best for a particular child's welfare. Whether this comes about through consultation with the adults involved, child focussed intervention, therapeutic work, assessment of child's abilities and needs or even looking for a diagnosis, I see the role of the educational psychologist as one which looks out for what is best for the child. The child is the practitioner's ultimate client – it is in the child's best interests that the practitioner maintains positive relationships with teachers, parents and other professionals. I am not saying that this is an easy stance to take since it brings out all sorts of dilemmas. There is no guide towards children's best welfare and sometimes judgements have to be made which are frightening (as mentioned in the previous chapter on uncertainty). The psychologist's recommendation may make life immediately harder for a child, for example in the case of behaviour difficulties or severe specific learning difficulties, but it would be seen as possibly helping the child in the future. The child's motivation and willingness to work has to be balanced with the need for hard work. While a child is still motivated, then more than half the battle is won.

Thus I want to explore the educational psychologist's role as one which aims to look out for what is best for the child. This presents difficulties for the practitioner for a number of reasons. The most obvious one is that it is not always clear what the best for a child is, and different agents in a situation may have different views on this issue. Another point, however, is that such a purpose is normally one for parents, as they are the ones on whom society can most depend to have the motivation and self-sacrificing attitude which such an aim may require. It may happen though that this falls through and society is called upon to provide that which a child's parents for some reason or another cannot give. It is possible that a psychologist is asked to intervene, besides the possibility of a social worker, a learning/behaviour support teacher, and any other professional whose intervention is deemed as useful for the child. We are called in because the more conventional institutions set up to see to the child's welfare, namely the family and the school, require the support of such professionals. We are called, on the surface, to support others in thinking of the child's welfare and best interests.

Now I see an inherent contradiction in this situation, and feel its effects constantly in my professional practice. As mentioned above, the educational psychologist is called upon to intervene in a situation where a child is experienced as difficult, in one way or another, by the persons around. Whether the location of the difficulty is rightly located within the child or not, the educational psychologist is asked for support in such a situation. These situations concern the child's happiness, education, and well-being. Probably, that child's relationships are brought up and questioned too. The contradiction is in the fact that the practitioner is asked to bring her professional self (the public self) to such a situation. The difficulty is presented when one thinks of the educational psychologist as a professional, possibly with boundaries around what belongs to the professional life and what belongs to the personal life. But when one tries to look out for a child's welfare, it would be a contradiction to make conditions around that role. It would be utterly contradictory to say that one wants to look out for children's welfare, provided that it does not impinge upon the professional's personal life. And yet, this is what we say, and also what we act out, in our daily life. The public (professional) life of the psychologist has to deal with the private life of the child.

> For the task that we undertake when working with children is nothing less than to negotiate as part of the web of society the boundaries between the private and the public; not just in lives of these young people but in our own (Billington, 2006, p. 162).

I am by no means saying that practitioners should not have their own personal life. Besides being quite ridiculous to expect a practitioner to dedicate herself completely to the children at work, it would also ensure that such a practitioner would have a very short working life owing to the burnout which would be guaranteed. However, we sometimes put on the child the unreasonable demand that the child confides in us and trusts us, while our presence has boundaries which we do not want the child to infringe. If the child asks too much, perhaps placing the question in the form of some 'unacceptable behaviour', then we have to resist, and say that the child requires support which is beyond us. We do not say that we are at fault because we cannot give the child our *personal* self – we say that the child is asking too much.

3. KEEPING THE PROFESSIONAL SELF AND THE PERSONAL SELF SEPARATE

It is apparent that there is a variety of perceptions of whether, and in what manner, one should reconcile one's personal and professional life. I argue that the practitioner is not a better professional because her personal life is left out of the picture. This may well be a question of definition and meanings. A person may be perceived as more professional because she does what needs to be done, regardless of the emotions which are involved. This stance may be important in certain situations and with specific professions. However, in the area of educational psychology and other caring professions, I argue that when a practitioner takes her emotions into consideration, this is a better indication of her professionalism than otherwise.

It is important that the personal and the professional be less firmly distinct as it would allow the practitioner to work with uncertainty, rather than to strive to remove it. In Chapters 10 and 11, I question the practices of practitioners in institutions, which institutions have policies and procedures which should be followed to ensure the streamlined functioning of a service. Such practices are present so that the contingencies of particular cases do not influence the action of the practitioner. Such procedures aim to give certainty in situations, which are problematic and messy, and practitioners, myself included, are often grateful that certain difficult decisions are taken out of their hands. As professionals, we are expected to abide by the policies of the institutions within which we practice. However, the 'intrusion' of the personal self does not, I argue, allow for the unquestioning adoption of the policies and procedures (see also Billig's (1988) contrary themes mentioned in Chapter 3). The personal self may be able to acknowledge more easily that there is not one rational answer in terms of Hollway's (1994) non-unified sense of the self. Uncertainty is more permissible with the personal self.

An example of this occurred a while ago during my involvement with a four year old child. I had been seeing Noel for over a year, since he was barely three years old. I attended his play school, observed and played with him at home and also watched several of the sessions which he had with his individual home tutor. I had just told Noel's mother that I believed that he did have a few autistic traits, but added that these were not the sole cause of Noel's behaviour. His father, who was separated from his mother, lived abroad and only saw his son for a few days every six weeks. Noel was starting to realise that his father did not magically appear and disappear every so often – he started to develop a sense of time and thus started to feel his father's absence more strongly and to play up when his father left the country.

Noel would be quite unsettled during the week after his father's departure, after which he would settle down to his mother's consistent routine once more. By saying that I believed that Noel's behaviour was partly owing to the destabilising effect of his father's coming and going, I did not want to blame Noel's dad, but wanted to explain the reasons for his behaviour.

Both parents seemed to accept my thoughts when I tentatively put these forward. I told them that it was difficult to be certain, especially as Noel was so young. Since I felt that I had a good idea about the dynamics of the family and had let both my professional as well as personal self get involved, I felt I could share the uncertainty with them. Noel did seem to have autistic traits, but the fact that he was a naturally active child and also the lack of routine when his father was around, also helped aggravate his behaviour. Thus I could not say which of these was the primary cause of the behavioural difficulties, which he presented to his mother. I also thought that deciding what was the primary cause was not necessary. I did not want the search for the diagnosis to take precedence over what was beneficial for the child.

Of course, this did not happen as easily as I am writing it. I had several qualms and asked myself whether I was just reluctant to diagnose autism to parents who seemed to have enough on their plate without adding further anxiety. Through the ideas which I am experimenting with, however, I found that Bannister's (1981 in Mellor, 1998) circumspection phase allowed me to think creatively. The conditioning with which we work, in which certainty is sought after, would mean a hasty precipitate diagnosis. Because I allowed my personal self to participate in my work with Noel, I was able to work with my uncertainty and to see multi-facets of Noel's difficulties and those of his parents. I also believe that, with this approach, it was easier for me to talk to the parents about how they contributed to his behavioural difficulties – I believe, also, that it may have been easier for them to take what I was saying on board. The tentative nature of my suggestions may have made it easier for them to evaluate what I was saying without feeling blamed.

It was thought best if Noel and his parents joined a non-governmental organisation which would provide regular sessions for Noel and also support the parents in their decisions regarding his schooling etc. I had recommended this move to the parents, warning them, however, that the organisation would insist on making their own assessment and diagnosis of his needs. Noel's mother called saying that following an hour of talking to the psychologist, who at the same time watched Noel in an unfamiliar room with toys, Noel was pronounced as having full-blown autism. The head of the organisation apologetically told Noel's mother that there was a short waiting list to join the programme which the organisation offered to children with this diagnosis. For the purposes of the organisation, Noel had autism – he fitted in that programme.

While, as already mentioned in Chapter 6, "a selective reduction of emotion is at least as prejudicial for rationality as excessive emotion" (Damasio, 1999, p. 41), reason and judgement do gain from operating using emotion. Awareness and an acknowledgement in the practitioner of her feelings allows for better practice with people. Since the sense impressions (already explained in terms of Bion's beta and alpha elements in the previous chapter) will invariably be present in the practitioner's experience, it is, I have argued, good practice not to resist them but to involve them judiciously in one's work.

An example comes to mind of an educational psychologist who recounted to me that he had just heard that morning that one of the children in his caseload had just died – the child had had severe disabilities and it seemed to have been expected. I believe that the fact that the psychologist was mentioning it to me showed that this event had left an impression on him, thus managing to penetrate his personal self. However, there was a limit as to how much this psychologist was prepared to allow this to affect him and to influence his actions:

> I recall a psychologist once telling me (when I asked how his day had been) that one of the pupils, whom he had been monitoring in a special school, had passed away the day before. He heard about this when he went to the school that day for another case. When asked whether he spoke to the bereaved family, he took a step back and raised his hand as though a policeman stopping cars, saying 'no, no…professional distance you know' (Conversion paper, 2004).

I believe that the expression that a person can put her heart and soul into work is not an exaggeration. When a professional decides to work with children with the intention of doing something to make changes for the better, there has to be that person's self in the professional self. This means that the professional has a stake in what she is investing so much energy into. Success, or even mere fulfilment and completion of one's intentions, will not only mean that something positive was done for the people one works with, but will also mean the validation and reinforcement of one's self. In Chapter 10, MacIntyre's (2000) idea of the goods which help the person towards fulfilment is explained. For now, it should suffice to say that when a professional reflects on how to be a good practitioner, she is thus also reflecting on how to be a good person.

Another argument which is in favour of the acknowledgment of the personal is one which says that the personal is everywhere and we delude ourselves if we think that we have left it at home and are working with our professional self only. It might be that we think we can repress personal feelings and "be professional" about the children we come across. For one thing, I believe that our work would be very much the poorer for it, and also, I do not think that this is possible. In the same way that I wrote about immediacy in the previous chapter, the therapeutic element in our work should always be present (Hollway, 1994; Hollway and Jefferson, 2001). Therapeutically, our private self is always with us – it would be best to acknowledge it and use it to our best advantage and to the advantage of the children and adults we work with.

CONCLUSION

The uncertainty advocated in this book also allows for subversion and irony both in situations and with the self so that the rigid bureaucracy is questioned and perhaps even mistrusted. The story of Gemma in the next chapter is one example of the importance of such a role. This separation of the professional and the personal may be what sometimes gets in the way of the best welfare of the child, as the good of the service which one represents overrides the good of the child. This is of course not deliberately done – very often what happens is that if one were to point at the origin of the problematic situation, several professionals would feel very uncomfortable indeed. It is thus safer for all if the cause of the problem was the child – if she (in the case of Gemma) were to be put away and 'fixed', then everybody would feel reinforced and validated in their own position and role. The sad reality is that although this would very much be a matter of perception and attribution, rather than of truth, still the difference would be felt. Thus in the story of Gemma, although I feel she was wrongly blamed for the problems in her family and at school, she was going to be sent away to a residential school. I am sure that because the adults perceived her as the problem, their perception of the situation after she left would be a positive one, and would act upon it, thus reinforcing such perception. In their minds, therefore, the idea that Gemma was the origin of their difficulties would be reinforced.

CHAPTER 8

MEETING GEMMA

This chapter tells the story of my involvement with Gemma, which story has two phases. It starts with an initial interaction with Gemma, her family and her school. The next phase concerns the meeting of professionals which took place so that Gemma's next placement could be decided. Nagel's (2002) writing is used to help elicit the questions and reflections from the above story. As already noted in the introduction, the stories and vignettes used in this book, while intentionally chosen for their poignancy, are still typical examples of cases which educational psychologists and other helping professionals come across in day to day practice, as many colleagues would testify.

1. MEETING GEMMA

My analysis was that Gemma was misunderstood and rendered a scapegoat by the school and her family. She was the middle child in a family of six children and she somehow kept being blamed for all the family's troubles. Her behaviour was unmanageable and she really succeeded in instilling fear in the hearts of her school teachers so that the only foreseeable way forward seemed to them to be her permanent exclusion from the school. According to the referral, she had been referred for support in school at least four years prior to this incident and somehow this had just not been taken up. When she entered the room that I was sitting in, her whole demeanour and facial expression indicated that she strongly felt she had been wronged and picked on. I had already spoken to her teacher and the deputy head of school, both of whom had said that they had done their utmost to help her to no avail. Of course, they knew that I was there to try and see whether there was something else that they could do and were determined to let me know that Gemma was unreachable and that the only way forward was out. When speaking to Gemma I tried to impart to her that she had an ally in me, someone who would help her by translating her hurt and angry feelings into something that the grown ups could understand. I wanted her to feel that she was being given a chance, but a chance in which it was believed that she could succeed, not one which everybody seemed to contribute to setting yet another scene in which she would fail miserably. What I asked from her was that she would give me a chance to do so.

I negotiated with her, with her mother and with her teacher and I tried to induce them to offer an olive branch to each other. Gemma was not attending school in the afternoons because of her behaviour and she wished that she could stay on for that day. After all the expressions of goodwill expressed by the teacher, I did not think that she would refuse when I added my plea to Gemma's – I thought that their aim was to get her on their side – to have her understand that they cared for her and wanted her to be happy at school. But the teacher said that she did not think that Gemma deserved to be allowed to stay at school, considering what she did that day to the other children in class. Gemma's facial expression reverted once more to the way it had been when she first entered the room.

> The school didn't want Gemma to stay for the afternoon session – she had been missing them for 2 weeks. Gemma wanted to stay for that day and, because she had thumped a girl and really insulted the teacher, she wasn't going to be allowed to. Gemma was really miserable and cowed as she left the school premises with her weeping mother. I felt miserable and felt also responsible because I didn't manage to convince the school to have her stay, although I offered to stay with her until the end of the school day. Now they have half term and, although I shouldn't be working, I am going for a home visit and am thinking of doing some solution-focused work with her. I think that they have focused on the problem long enough – it's about time that we thought about the solution now (Journal: February, 2003).

Solution-focussed brief therapy is a term, coined in 1982, to describe an approach which is based on the realisation that focusing on the client's difficulties in therapy uses up the time, resources and energy which could be used to help arrive at solutions (Walter and Peller, 1992). The idea behind it is that by focusing on the moments when a client's difficulties are less or absent, awareness is brought on those moments so that clients are encouraged to repeat their successful actions, thus gaining confidence and hope in themselves and their life. I felt very unsure about what my best move with Gemma should be and felt so bogged down by the difficulties listed that I thought that this approach would help us all focus on the few positive moments. However, the professionals working in school seemed to be beyond this point. I did not know how I could move them to realise that meeting Gemma half way was not going to work. Gemma needed to see them go completely out of their way before she would concede they cared a jot about her. On the other hand, I tried very hard to persuade the teacher that I understood that her intentions were to teach Gemma and that she tried to help her – but it was a question of how Gemma perceived her actions. I was also conscious that the teacher might think that it was easy for me to think about Gemma in these terms, never having yet spent six hours with her class day in day out. I wanted the teacher to know that I understood her point of view – but at the same that we had to move on.

> The solution-focussed work is just something to do – what I want to do is let her think that somebody cares and somebody wants her to be ok, not necessarily happy, just ok. No matter what the reality is, if she thinks she is given a chance, then her outlook and perception will change. The school thinks that they are giving her chances but her perception of them nullifies their potential. The teacher was offended when I told her that Gemma's perceiving her as spiteful – she understood eventually that I was talking about perception and then seemed to take what I was saying and suggesting on board (Journal: February, 2003).
>
> While her teacher is trying to get through to Gemma, she is not realising that Gemma might be trying to get through to her also – and the teacher might be

> just as impenetrable as Gemma is. In the same way as Gemma not letting the teacher come through to her with her rudeness and inappropriate behaviour – the teacher might be as inaccessible to her because of her teacherish attitude. She can say she's ok because she can see that she gets on well with most other people in her life. But unlike Gemma, the teacher's influence on Gemma's life is not merely restricted to the classroom. Gemma cannot go and tell on the teacher that she's been picking on Gemma – but the teacher can. Her home life won't be influenced by exclusion or by a teacher's report. But Gemma's will be – Gemma's mother cries because of her and her little sister acts 'mum' towards her in a way that is intolerable. Her elder brother picks on her horribly. No wonder that Gemma is only lovable with her cat and with Fred, her little brother who has quite significant needs himself (Journal: February, 2003).

> When I have Gemma and her teacher both in front of me and I speak to the child and tell her what is being suggested and ask what she thinks about it, the child replies in an uncooperative way. And I think that is quite acceptable and expected from someone who has become accustomed to being put down and who reacts in such a way which is calculated to frustrate the person perceived as threatening. The problem is when the teacher intervenes and tries to convince the child that her behaviour is unacceptable and of course Gemma is not going to listen to more of that. She feels betrayed by me also, because I seem to have trapped her into yet another situation where she has to hear what she's done wrong and how she's 'got to act' in order to put things right (Journal: March, 2003).

On the same day, while walking out of the school, I met the deputy head of the school and was quite shocked to realise that the way the school was seeing Gemma was such that the behaviour exhibited was almost expected, because they believed she had quite significant needs. Both Gemma and the school seemed to be dancing around each other in a vicious circle of expectations. While Gemma expected the school to let her down, she acted in such a way as to make sure that they did. While the school expected Gemma to misbehave, they acted towards her in such a way which provoked her worst attitude and behaviour.

> The deputy head has told me that she thinks Gemma's on the autistic spectrum, "because it can't just be ADHD because she's so bad". But autism isn't a degree worse than ADHD – it can be seen as being on the spectrum but is also a different thing. When I expressed this, she said "well it's either that or there's something mentally wrong with her". Oh my god – I felt shivers run down my spine. Is that the road we're going down now? What about the 6 years that Gemma's been in that school with no support? There needs to be time taken with Gemma – her trust needs to be gained and that takes time. It's the school's responsibility to provide for this (Journal: March, 2003).

My dilemma was that while I was strongly convinced that the school was not helping Gemma at all, I could not convey this to the adults working there as strongly as I felt it.

I wanted to persuade them of it, but my conviction would have alienated their already grudging support of me. As McNab (2001) was quoted in the previous chapter, Gemma was perceived to be the problem and the solution was to be obtained through a change in *her* attitudes, *her* perceptions and *her* demeanour, while they stood firm. The adults working in Gemma's school absolutely could not see themselves as the recipients of my service – they were just customers (McNab, 2005). Gemma's private self was being asked to conform to their professional selves. Yet, in accepting this, I was colluding and ran the risk of Gemma perceiving me as betraying her too. I could see myself in her eyes – I was setting her up for failure too. Billington also speaks of that moment of betrayal in his interaction with Gary's school teachers when confronted with determined application of authority and concludes: "Sorry Gary … I should have seen it coming … perhaps my resistance can be of little use to you if other, powerful professionals are too deeply committed to the pathology" (Billington, 2000, p. 17).

> How am I wronging Gemma? Am I underdiagnosing or am I being really insightful? To what extent can I collude with the teacher without betraying Gemma? I find myself apologising whenever I come up with suggestive comments to the teacher "Can you ask her how she feels about it and what she thinks about it?" Also when asked for suggestions about a meeting taking place between school, Gemma and mum while she was excluded, I said: "I don't think you'll get anywhere by laying down the law." I suggested: "Talk to Gemma and tell her that although it looks as though she might be changing school, tell her: we need to find a way of getting on together for these last four weeks. I know that it seems to you that I've been picking on you – which may be true because now you've got a reputation for misbehaving – but I would really like these last four weeks before the end of the Easter term to be better. How do you think this might best have a chance of happening?" That's what I told her to tell her. I was only told about this meeting on the morning of that day – and so couldn't attend it. I really hope that something happened – but Gemma is not going to make it easy for them to work with her and they don't seem to have the confidence in her to motivate them to keep on trying to work as partners with her (Journal: March, 2003).

Needless to say, even giving Gemma only four more weeks in school was too much to ask, both from her as well as from the school. To make matters worse, the school which we were hoping would give Gemma a second chance suddenly became an active player in the story. There was no way that this school was going to accept such a child. At that point, nobody wanted Gemma. She was asked to stay home by the school which currently had her written in their school register. But her mother found her too difficult to handle when she was at home all the time. Gemma was to be sent to a residential school, "where she might be helped to deal with her own behaviour and respite given to her family" (My report on Gemma, 2003).

Thus not only was Gemma seen as the scapegoat in school, but she was also seen as the cause of her family's difficulties. The solution was, to put it in crude terms, to pack Gemma off to a residential school and everyone would be happy again.

However, my reading of the situation was different in that I sympathised with Gemma's perception that she was very much picked on:

> …on one of the home visits, I saw Gemma being teased by Mark, her older brother, and also scolded by Tamara, and consequently saw Gemma start getting exasperated, frustrated and quite potentially aggressive. It seemed to me as though these little situations could get out of control very fast and indeed, Gemma was later blamed for her aggressive behaviour. There were a lot of things happening at the same time because Gemma's parents were telling her off while Mark was still teasing her, and I saw Gemma was progressively feeling rather cornered. I understood that since Gemma's parents have had quite violent behaviour from her frequently, they attempted to prevent such a situation from happening by dealing with Gemma straight away, whereas Gemma felt that her brother was the cause in this instance (Report on Gemma, 2003, p. 2).

2. THE MEETING OF PROFESSIONALS

A meeting was eventually called so that Gemma's placement could be decided upon. The meeting was attended by the girl's mother, the behaviour support teacher, social worker, community worker, the deputy head of school, the head of the nearby school (where she would attend if she were to be excluded from her present school), and members of the school council who were there to back the latter head of school in her refusal to admit Gemma. Everybody talked about this girl as being the source of all the problems caused in this family. They wanted to send her to a nearby residential school for children with behavioural difficulties. I felt very inadequate during this meeting as I tried to present her as a girl who was hurt and upset and, most of all, misunderstood. I was not taken very seriously and after some more discussion the meeting was adjourned until the following week.

I felt that I had let Gemma down and called the area senior educational psychologist in tears and explained to him that I had failed. He told me that that was not the way he saw the situation but that I was probably the only person in that meeting who had stood up for the girl. I had been confused and irritable at my lack of security but this apparent lack of confidence was really a hesitation to label the child negatively. It kept me from accepting what the others said would benefit the child. I did not agree with sending Gemma to a residential school for children with behavioural difficulties. The way that this action was put forward made it seem as though Gemma was being punished. It seemed unjust that Gemma should be made to take the blame for the failure of his family, school and the professionals who had entered the picture to help Gemma. Placing Gemma in this residential school, away from her little brother and cat whom she loved, would rid the school and her family of a problem. I could not say during the meeting that I was positive that the problems in Gemma's family would locate themselves elsewhere if Gemma was not around, that at the moment they were seen as solely caused by Gemma because she was the most vulnerable. Neither could I say that, seeing how the school dealt with Gemma's difficulties, I would not be surprised if the same happened to another child attending that school, once Gemma was not around to be blamed anymore. In the concluding paragraph of my report, I made a final effort to remove at least some of the allocated responsibility for the negative situation away from Gemma and towards the adults around her:

> School decisions about Gemma over recent months have inadvertently provided Gemma and her parents with incontrovertible evidence that she is not wanted. It is not surprising, therefore, that Gemma's behaviour has deteriorated (report on Gemma, 2003, p. 5).

And yet even here, I felt compelled to use the word *inadvertently* because I did not want to alienate the adults in the school too much. Yet nobody had any qualms about saying some quite horrible things about Gemma, sometimes even to her face. She had to take it – she had no choice – but there I was, the person whose role it was to be Gemma's advocate, trying to placate and sweet-talk her teachers. In terms of McNab's (2005) terminology of the different roles in the relationship network, Gemma ought to have been the Customer of my service, where this means that she is "asking the Service to undertake the piece of work in question" (point 3). She should be consulting with me about the Recipient, where this implies "the object – i.e. is on the receiving end – of an EPS (Educational Psychology Service) activity, whether they asked for it or not" (point 5). But, as the author of this document himself points out, "Young people (teenagers) are only very occasionally in a Customer relationship to Service activities, and younger children so extremely rarely as to be, for all practical purposes, never" (McNab, 2005, point 4).

I want to go back momentarily to the point made earlier about the contradiction in the situation where the private life of the child has to be dealt with by the professional life of the practitioner. This is precisely one of those situations. Gemma was not given a choice, but had to deal with me, and with her teachers. However, everything had to be done on my terms. Although I strongly sympathised with her, I had to deal with the adults myself and thus tried to make compromises. I had to be professional about it, while all the time realising how miserably I was short-changing this girl who was misunderstood by everybody. All she wanted was someone to believe in her and to be very very patient while she emerged from her protective hide. She needed a relationship with an adult – but the one I could offer her was limited. I had other children to see, I had my studies, I had my holidays. Gemma was only given a part of the professional part of my life, although I cannot deny that she had my personal sympathy throughout. Thus the answer to the question asked in my journal regarding whether and in what manner I was wronging Gemma, was the following:

> I feel I am wronging Gemma because I should be spending more time with her – take her out – make her feel valued and loved for what she is – show her that I think she's going to behave and that I'm not apprehensive of what she's going to do next. But that's not my role – it's their role and they're not doing it. What's your story going to be, Gemma, in four or five years' time? Maybe someone in secondary school will seem sympathetic towards you and will help you overcome this horrible self-image that others have of you and

that you, I think, have of yourself. I hope so, but I don't know (Journal: March, 2003).

The impact which my decisions will have on her life is enormous and far-reaching. Relatively speaking, the impact which she will have on my life is minimal. She will be a thought in my mind, at most, an incessant worry. Yet even this is grudged – we professionals tell each other that we have to leave our work behind when we go home – don't take your work worries with you. Yet on my suggestion, Gemma could physically be removed from her family and placed in a residential school. This is something which she will not be able to momentarily put away from her mind, as I am recommended to do, as a 'good professional' who knows boundaries.

3. MORALITY AS THE RESULT OF PREFERENCE

Here I would like to focus a bit more on the final meeting regarding Gemma's placement. I felt a deep dissatisfaction with the proceeding and outcome of the meeting and also felt ashamed of myself and of other the professionals in the helping professions as I perceived us all as putting up a pretence of trying to help Gemma.

In the aforementioned meeting regarding Gemma's future education, it seemed that everyone present was well rehearsed and prepared for the part she had to play. Files are even taken home the day before and read, and lunches are missed so that such meetings are adequately prepared for. Everybody seems tense just before the meeting and there is a lot of small talk before there is a clear sign that the meeting has begun. Then, once this happens and everything starts to be minuted, the rehearsed roles are played out. Arguments are weighed prior to being put forward for consideration - the person with such an argument gauges whether a moment would be best to put it forward, or whether it should be saved and deferred until it is needed against a strong antagonistic remark passed by another person at the meeting, whose aims for a child are different to one's own. Everybody seems to have hidden agendas but no one takes the responsibility of uncovering them – indeed they may be accepted as a reality. If one were brave enough to do so, one would then have to bear the consequences of handing the group discussion a live bomb which might explode and make everybody, including the child, the loser.

The outcome of such a situation, rather than it being rather obvious as to where Gemma would receive the best support, may depend on the statements of the person with the strongest character and ability to carry her argument well. The capacity to make oneself heard is a great asset, as is having a name for being able to have things one's way. I strongly believed at Gemma's meeting that my arguments would have been better presented had the senior educational psychologist done the talking - at the very least, they would have been better received by the rest of the group than the arguments of a newly qualified educational psychologist were. Is it possible then that a child's placement is decided upon very much like a football match, where many teams try to score a goal in anyone else's goal post? Can the decision of Gemma's placement be as contingent and coincidental as a goal in such a match? Did the child get the best deal, or did the loudest, most persuasive speech win through?

People leave this kind of meeting feeling satisfied, feeling that it went well, or feeling that they have lost the argument. The very fact that people have positive or negative views about how a meeting went, whether it is something which has finished, whether they have had their chance to air their opinions and perspective, is in itself very worrying. What would happen if someone found a new argument to present? Can that person ask for the meeting to re-convene, or has that person missed his chance? How important has new information got to be so that all the professionals meet again to sift through the arguments? Who makes this decision? Is it now considered too late, that enough time has been spent on this child and that it is time to move on to the next?

Thus perhaps, the difficulty which permeates such situations as I have described above is that we see our role as different in different situations. It seems that we manage to cut up our life into partitions and segments, and relegate each with its own norms and appropriate modes of behaviour. If during a meeting, the aim of each professional is to meet the expectations of her own service, then, considering the limitations of that service and need to safeguard the well-being of its workers by guarding against overwork, the professional would be motivated to uphold the maxim that what is required of the meeting is to ensure that *adequate* provision is given to the child. If, however, the aim is to see the best provision for a child, then, adequate simply is not enough anymore. This creates complications, and thus causes some practitioners to maintain that it is the parent's role to look out for the best of the child. However, sometimes, parents fail their children for a variety of reasons which may even be out of their control and professionals may be called upon. The different roles are believed to provide what is best for the child. However, while theoretically this seems to add up, in reality it does not happen this way.

Nagel (2002) writes about the complexity of decisions and judgements and says that one of the marks of humanity is "the capacity to view the world simultaneously" (p. 134) from a variety of points of view. He claims that there is a great division between five fundamental types of value, which value gives rise to basic conflict. There is no comparing of these sources of value so that when a judgement is passed, this will mean "acting against some reasons without being able to claim that they are *outweighed*" (p. 129).

> The great division between personal and impersonal, or between agent-centred and outcome-centred, or subjective and objective reasons, is so basic that it renders implausible any reductive unification of ethics – let alone of practical reasoning in general. The formal differences among these types of reasons correspond to deep differences in their sources (p. 133).

The five fundamental types of value of which Nagel (2002) writes can easily be located in various parts of the story recounted in this chapter. Earlier in the previous chapter I suggest that the role of educational psychologist is to look out for the best welfare of the child, while in this story there is an issue about whether the professionals in the meeting were doing so, or rather looking out for the interests of the service which they represented. This is a conflict, as Nagel (2002) explains, within his first (though not in importance) category, comprised of specific obligations to other people and institutions. The next category is that of constraints on action deriving from general rights that everyone has. This was strongly felt by Gemma's school, which insisted upon certain behaviour from her, notwithstanding her perceived hurts. Gemma's teacher insisted that she could not continue to act and treat others in such a manner without feeling the consequences of her actions. Third is the consideration of the effects of what one does on everyone's welfare. The school administration was adamant that Gemma could not continue to attend that school, as her presence endangered the other children, especially those in her class. Furthermore, during the meeting of the various professionals involved with Gemma and her family, the perceived effects of Gemma's actions on her immediate family were given great importance and served to be one of the main motivators of the arguments in favour of placing Gemma in a residential school.

The fourth category in Nagel's (2002) list consists of perfectionist ends and values. I believe that this was the part which I played in the story, as I strongly felt the injustice which was being done to Gemma in putting on her the blame of everybody's difficulties, and thus would not agree with the proposed solution. It is possible that, considering the mind sets of the various actors close to Gemma, the proposed solution was a practical one, which might have served everybody's purpose, perhaps even Gemma. However, I could not accept that Gemma was going to be sent away, as though in punishment, when I believed that there were many who had contributed to constructing Gemma in her destructive role.

The final category is that of commitment to one's own projects or undertakings. "It is partly a matter of justifying earlier investment of time and energy, and not allowing it to have been in vain. It is partly a desire to be the sort of person who finishes what he begins. But whatever the reason, our projects make autonomous claims on us, once undertaken, which they need not have made in advance" (Nagel, 2002, p. 130). I believe that, in this story, all the actors, including myself, did not want to concede to others the intentions which accompanied us to the meeting. There seemed to be a personal stake in the argumentation going on.

So what would it mean to give a system of priorities among the fundamental types of value? The fact that Nagel believes that value has fundamentally different kinds of sources, "does this mean, then, that basic conflicts have no solution?" (2002, p. 134). What Nagel contends is that judgement, described as practical wisdom (or phronesis) by Aristotle, makes it possible for decision-making to take place, notwithstanding the difficulties. Although one may not be able to justify completely a decision taken, although one cannot say why a certain decision is a correct one, it does not mean that there cannot be a claim to correctness. This practical wisdom is revealed through individual decision in practice rather than in the articulation of general principles. Although this practical wisdom may not yield a solution which satisfies every requirement in a situation and may not even emerge as a confident judgement owing to the complexities which the practitioner becomes aware of, still "in many cases it can be relied on to take up the slack that remains beyond the limits of explicit rational argument" (Nagel, 2002, p. 135). I want to point out here a note mentioned earlier, in Chapter 3, when the contingent nature of any decision and judgement is explained by Derrida, who quotes Kierkegaard saying that a decision is a madness

(Derrida, 1992, p. 26). Nagel (2002), however, seems to maintain that through this practical wisdom, the arbitrariness of the decision-making moment is catered for. In enunciating this point, Nagel (2002) makes it possible for the practitioner to proceed in her work, making decisions while still acknowledging uncertainty, without however, stepping into irresponsibility and irrationality.

> Provided one has taken the process of practical justification as far as it will go in the course of arriving at the conflict, one may be able to proceed without further justification, but without irrationality either (ibid., p. 135).

CONCLUSION

This chapter concludes by introducing the final theme of this book, that of practical judgement which follows throughout the next three chapters. The story of Gemma was told in this chapter so that the dilemma of personal and professional self may be put in a context of practice. This led to a discussion of the ability to have simultaneous perspectives of the world as a mark of humanity, as pointed out by Nagel (2002). The latter suggests that the fragmentation is brought together in practical dilemmas through the application of practical wisdom, which point will be further expanded on in the following chapters.

> Most practical decisions are much messier than this, and their ethical dimensions are much more complex.... But for most of the questions that need deciding, ethical considerations are multiple, complex, often cloudy, and messed up with many others. They need to be considered in a systematic way, but in most cases a reasonable decision can be reached only by sound judgement, informed as well as possible by the best arguments that any relevant disciplines have to offer (Nagel, 2002, p. 141).

CHAPTER 9

MEETING ALEXANDRA

The next three chapters aim to address dilemmas by directly focussing on professionalism. Whereas in Chapters 4, 5 and 6 the issue of uncertainty was explored with reference to scientific truth in research and practice, and in Chapters 7 and 8 the values with which professionals work were looked into, here I would like to problematise professionalism with regards to practice in the caring professions.

The following arguments aim to explore some of the issues incumbent in professionalism, and to question them with regards to the qualities expected from a professional and the contradictions that there might be between the claims of the profession and those of the institution. I introduce these issues through the story of Alexandra, an eight year old girl who was referred to me for special examination arrangements as she was sitting for an exam the results of which would place her in a particular stream in the following years of schooling.

This chapter tells the story of my involvement with a child and her mother. Alexandra was one in my list of children whom I had to assess for the purpose of providing support during examinations. The subsections address the context of the story, and then the details of how my involvement progressed, first with Alexandra's mother and then with her. The focus of the story is very much on my progression in the case as the story unfolded and as I deliberated about which course of action was best for Alexandra's well-being. The eventual outcomes of the story are also outlined.

1. CONTEXT OF MY INVOLVEMENT WITH ALEXANDRA AND HER MOTHER

While in training, every time I heard of what were termed as exam dispensations, I noticed that my educational psychologist colleagues would groan, roll their eyes and make facial and verbal expressions of disgust and boredom. I quickly learned that these exam dispensations were regarded as the bane of EP existence, as the exercise was described as a mere administrative and bureaucratic one, where the educational psychologist's role was to make a recommendation for some arrangement to take place in exams to remove the disadvantages incurred through specific learning difficulties. This cannot be done in an automatic way, so that one cannot simply allocate a particular support to a particular specific learning difficulty. The way this had to happen was that the support would be provided for the child, keeping in mind that child's difficulties, but also in the context of her individual abilities. The importance of the uniqueness of each case is still maintained, although the manner in which such cases are allocated to an educational psychologist make it difficult for her to treat them as such. It is enough to mention that these cases arrive to the psychologist in bulk and thus somehow lose their individuality. It is easy to refer to the ever-growing pile as 'exam dispensations' and to forget we are still referring to children and their needs. It is very tempting to regard such referrals as a chore.

While on training I attended a seminar given to the educational psychologists who were my supervisors, which seminar dealt with the new formation that examination dispensations had to have. The non-complex cases were to be tackled at school level with specialist teachers to support the Special Educational Needs Coordinators in making their recommendations. The only cases which educational psychologists were to become involved in were those which were deemed to be complicated. It seemed to be an arrangement which my colleagues liked, as it would allow them to focus better on those cases which required greater thought and delicate handling. This would be owing either to the particular impairment which the child in question had, or to cases in which it was difficult to decide on what support to give, especially if the school and parents disagreed on what would best serve the child without being unfair (although everyone agreed that examinations and fairness do not go as hand in hand as the system would make us believe). However, in the scenario of this particular story, there is a different state of affairs. The stakes are considerably higher, as the result of the exam determines which stream a child attends the following year.

There is great pressure on teachers, parents and children during these years, and the examination can be seen to be the epitome of performativity. Teachers are said to be good at their job or not, depending on how many of the children in their class pass the exam. Parents seem to feel that they are failing their children if the life of the whole family does not rotate around the child who is sitting for this exam. Television programmes are aired every year around May and June, which are dedicated to this national phenomenon: examinations which stream children. Horrifying tales are proudly told by parents who actually make their children study until the small hours of the night, in an attempt to secure a place for their children in a higher stream.

If there is a chance that a child might merit some special consideration during exams because of a specific learning difficulty, or for some other reason, then it stands to reason that parents will apply for it, sometimes at the risk of pathologising the children. In most of the cases in which an application for special examination arrangements is submitted, the claim is judged as founded and some sort of provision is made. However, in a small understaffed Service which is increasingly struggling to cope with the demand, these applications may be perceived as energy taken away from the work which could be done with individual clients.

There is a lot of pressure to meet deadlines. At the same time, notwithstanding this and also the fact that such work is frequently monotonous, there is the ongoing debate about whether we still ought to try our best to see each individual case on its own merit and to give due consideration to its complexity or to simply treat it as an SEA (Special Examination Arrangements) case. It is very difficult to stop myself from seeing this group of clients in terms of numbers and as I close each file and turn to open another, I hear myself mentally shout the word "next!" in a bored and detached voice, as they do in films. The sad part of this is that when we come across a case which is immediately striking because it is more convoluted and complex, then we do not have the time to cater for such a case properly. If we do so, we are conscious that we are neglecting other cases, who are also equally worthy, because all cases deserve attention. If what I mentioned above was the 'sad part', what I will mention now is the part which frightens me: what about those cases which are *not* 'immediately striking', but are still convoluted and complex? In the 'sad part' we at least know of their existence; in the 'frightening part' we have no knowledge of them.

2. INTRODUCING ALEXANDRA THROUGH HER MOTHER'S ACCOUNT

Alexandra was the first child I encountered through the Special Examination Arrangements route. I went to the school, planning to see four children and their parents and thus 'deal with four SEAs in one morning' – the expression implies a sense of efficiency and effectiveness although this is no excuse for the lack of individuality. I went to the primary school and met Alexandra's mother for the first time. She did not strike me to be in any way remarkable. She told me that her concerns about Alexandra were mostly in maths as she is sometimes difficult to motivate academically. I listened to her almost automatically, still conscious of the list of parents and children which I had to see that day. She then said that Alexandra lost her father earlier that year – that caught my attention! I seemed to see her again for the first time as I expressed my sympathy for their loss with genuine feeling.

Alexandra's mother said that her husband had been ill for a long time, in fact for six years, and that she had accompanied him abroad several times for his hospitalisation. I asked her whether a family relative had looked after Alexandra and her elder sister on these visits and she replied that she had no one to help her look after the children. They were placed in a children's home for months at a time. As I empathised with her, she continued, saying that the children had suffered too, particularly Alexandra. Whereas in the first home where they had stayed, both children were well looked after and happy, after a few visits, this home was too full of children and their mother had to leave them at a much larger children's home. Here the children had some negative experiences with the other children. Alexandra used to come back home quite an angry girl, quick tempered and aggressive sometimes. She had also contracted a skin condition which required some quite painful treatment.

Seeing the children suffer like this, Alexandra's father refused to have his wife accompany him to England again when next he went. Although he had been told that this would probably be the last treatment he would have, he went alone and did not tell his wife that he had been told that those were his last months of life. All this was recounted to me by Alexandra's mother in a calm sorrowful way but the room felt heavy with memories. I had stopped writing by this time and just looked at her, following her through her story. I came home later and sat down and just wrote and wrote – it affected me so much.

I expressed to her mother that it was no wonder that Alexandra was finding it difficult to concentrate, considering that her grief was so fresh and also considering her experiences in the children's home. Her mother agreed and said that she was really a wonderful child – she was kind hearted and had many interests. However, while Alexandra's sister's school performance was not affected by these difficulties, Alexandra's exam marks were decreasing considerably.

As the mother continued to tell me how worried she had been about Alexandra for numerous times of her life, she said that even when she was only one year old she had been very ill, and mentioned as an aside that she had been adopted. I felt as though the ground was completely pulled from under my feet! I exclaimed as she told me the dire condition that Alexandra was in when she was adopted. She was very ill, severely undernourished and had undergone some physical abuse. She required hospitalisation but the mother pleaded with doctors to let her take Alexandra home from hospital so that she could care for her until she was healthy again. They reluctantly conceded and, with pride in her voice, she told me how she had managed to make Alexandra healthy and strong again. The family settled for what they believed would be a normal family life, just like the one everyone else had. Within a year, her husband was diagnosed with cancer.

I looked at her with sympathy and respect and promised her that I would do everything I could to help Alexandra. She was grateful as she told me that although she wished Alexandra to achieve good results in these exams, she had also tried to have Alexandra enter a smaller school where a closer watch could be placed on children in terms of pastoral care, which would mean that she would not have to sit for the very selective exams. For Alexandra to have such special consideration, a psychologist's report was required, in which the reasons for which I considered that she merited such consideration were to be written. This was a difficult report to write, as I had to put forward my case in such a way that would convince the gate-keeping authorities that Alexandra should be given a place in a selective smaller school. I promised Alexandra's mother that I would do my best and said that I would write the report, following my assessment of Alexandra, to support her application – in a smaller school where the emphasis on pastoral care was strong, Alexandra would be monitored and supported better and I had no qualms about supporting her. And I had not yet met Alexandra. The following are excerpts of my writing following this meeting:

> One would never think, when one goes to a school to see parents and children for Special Examination Arrangements that one would hear a story like this. I went to Haz-Zghir to see the children. I had asked Mrs Borg the assistant head to make the appointments for me. We had an urgent meeting at work the first time we had to meet and our appointment was cancelled. Then Mrs Borg made the appointments and I barely knew the names of the children whom I was going to see. I arrived about 5 minutes late, armed with my test. Alexandra was the only child who had not ever been assessed and I thus had to conduct an assessment of her needs and abilities so that I could recommend SEAs.
>
> Her mother was there, waiting for me. Mrs Borg introduced us and we shook hands. We were taken to the clinic and we sat down, exchanging small talk. She was a very serious woman; she seemed old to be parent to an eight year old child. Then she started to tell me that Alexandra was worrying her because her marks deteriorated radically last annual exams. She mentioned, it seemed as though in passing, that her husband died recently; she then added that it was after six years of being ill with cancer. She then said that the children

had to stay in a home while they were away for treatment. As an aside, she said that the children had been adopted and that they had come to her and her husband from very bad conditions.

I couldn't catch up with her. I stopped trying to take notes and stared at her flabbergasted, asking and exclaiming with each tragedy. She had me totally with her. Everything, all the SEAs, all the waiting list, the urgent list, the school, my own life, faded away as I listened to what this woman was telling me. In the children's home, Alexandra and her sister had caught some infections. They had been very unhappy there. Their behaviour was not good at all. They were unkempt and dirty. Their mother spoke with some anger as she said that she had provided for the children's care while they were in the home.

I wanted to promise her everything she wanted. I wanted to give her special exam arrangements and I spoke to her about family therapy for her and the children so that they could get help through their bereavement. It was good that she was attending a support group, and that the children enjoyed it when she took them with her on outings. It was also striking that she knew just how sad the story was. She said that when she spoke at the support group they told her that they cannot say their story because it was nothing compared to hers. And yet it came out so simply from her mouth when she recounted it to me – without any attempt at sensationalism. There was some pride when she spoke – it seemed to be at the extent of their suffering. But then again, it was not pride, it was resignation, without emotion. She had gone through it, it was over and now it was her task to pull the family together, to fit the pieces, to see to her children's needs. What a formidable woman… (Journal: December 12, 2004).

3. MEETING ALEXANDRA

Alexandra was as beautiful a child as her mother described her. She was eager and quiet and enjoyed getting to know me and telling me about her. When asked about her father, Alexandra did not find it difficult to disclose her feelings and we spoke at some length about her sadness and concerns about this experience. I described my work to her and explained the assessment process. She was ready to start and we set off, starting with the Recall of Design and then the Word Definition subtests of the Differential Ability Scales (Elliott, 1990). As I asked her to describe the words to me, alarm bells started ringing in my head when she explained the word 'plan' to me by saying that she sometimes planned her own death when she was angry at something. They rang louder when she tried to explain the word 'curiosity' by saying that she was curious about her father's stay at the Intensive Care Unit in hospital and eventual death there. Alexandra seemed to be very preoccupied with death and dying and even mentioned the time when she was an infant and she was close to death as she had heard the story from her mother. Her unanswered questions about her father's illness and about people's vulnerability in general gave her cause for concern. In fact, during my assessment, our interaction very frequently rotated around these issues, as she obviously had thoughts and questions which she needed to answer and resolve.

However, I started to get very concerned when she described to me some moments when she had contemplated her own death. One particular incident occurred when she was playing with a ball on the roof of their house and the ball went over the little wall surrounding the roof. There was a narrow ledge beyond this wall and Alexandra went on it to retrieve her ball, which had not fallen down. She described to me that when she found herself on this ledge, with nothing between her and the drop, she had a funny feeling and thought that she could easily jump at that moment and be with her father in heaven. I listened to her with my hair standing on edge. In as calm a voice as possible, I asked her whether she had ever told her mother about these thoughts, to which she replied that she had not, because she did not want to worry her.

> I told her that I had to tell her mother this – I had not spoken to her about confidentiality before – didn't think to do so since this was about SEAs. She was dismayed and asked me why I felt I had to do so. She said "Is it because you think it will happen to me?" I felt slightly reassured because she spoke of it in a way which showed her perception of death being an external thing, which 'happened' to one. I told her that I wasn't afraid that this would happen to him but explained to her that when children told us such things, it meant that they really were feeling sad. I said that we got worried when children felt so sad and so we always tell their parents to make sure that the people around them know and can look after them (Journal: December 12, 2004).

I found myself in quite a tight spot with Alexandra because I felt that in all honestly I had to let this unsuspecting confiding girl know that I had to inform her mother about her thoughts. I was glad that I gave her an explanation, which did not sound accusatory, or one, which could make her feel found out. However, at the same time I still felt that I was somehow betraying her, albeit for her own safety and well-being. I was angry with myself for not making sure that I was covered in terms of the boundaries of the confidentiality issue and felt that I had let myself walk straight into a dilemma which could have easily been avoided.

And yet could it? Had I forewarned Alexandra that there were certain things which I could not keep to myself, would that make it all above board and honest? I cannot talk about this situation as though this were a contract and there was some small writing which I was to put in at the bottom of the page, just to make sure that I was 'covered'. To start with, what does forewarning Alexandra mean? She could interpret it as me letting her know that there were things which she might tell me which I could not, or would not, handle and would blow the whistle on her (McNamee, 2001, p. 423). Furthermore, it is ridiculous to have the idea that had Alexandra been told this, she would have understood what it signified and known what to do about it and taken a decision about whether to speak or not.

On paper (to keep up the allegory of the contract), I was still bound to disclose – and yet I felt I was faced with a moral conflict. As McNamee discusses, "we need not assume that all moral conflicts are conflicts in the realm of duty. Most of us would recognise conflicts of value that fall short of conflicts of duty. And besides, in a complex predicament…, the distinction between moral and non-moral considerations may not be easy to draw" (2001, p. 429). I could not help feeling somewhat responsible for this situation. "Where we feel neither guilt nor regret in such a case, we display the moral callousness of indifference and insensitivity" (ibid., p. 437).

Being a sweet-natured child, Alexandra did not seem to take it against me although she was still unwilling for me to tell her mother. I tried to come to a compromise and told her that I would give her a chance to tell her mother herself. I said to her that I was coming to the school again in two weeks and would check with her mother to ensure that she had told her. She seemed relieved at this reprieve and agreed to my terms. We finished our assessment and parted on good terms, although I was, at the very least, much shaken by the morning's work.

4. THE DILEMMA

Alexandra was referred to us through the Special Examination Arrangements route and, according to procedure, I was supposed to refer her to a psychiatrist because she had morbid thoughts. Here again, I found myself in great conflict. Why was I finding it so hard to be the bearer of bad news? I did not want to tell Alexandra's mother that her troubles were not over because I was going to add to them my disclosure of what Alexandra had told me and what I had to recommend in response. I wanted to reassure her that things were going to be all right, after a very difficult seven year experience of sickness, sorrow and loss.

Besides this, I was very frightened because I believed that, besides me needing to follow the procedure of referring to a psychiatrist in cases of potential suicide, there was a possibility of me being a party to pathologise what was simply a stage in Alexandra's grieving process. I questioned myself and my motives over and over again – again I had sleepless nights. In the end, I decided that I had to rely on the procedure because, if something had happened to Alexandra, then it would be my fault for not referring. When I decided this, I felt that I was possibly sacrificing Alexandra for my own protection. I still was not comfortable with my decision.

At the same time, I consulted with colleagues about this case and a discussion went on about whether, when we saw children through the SEA route, we ought to go into such issues with them. The majority agreed that we could not do otherwise, that we had to see all children on their own merit and not depending on the route through which they had been referred. However, we had qualms about those other children who had been waiting for our involvement for months and whom we still could not see.

The following are excerpts of my writing at this stage of my involvement with this case.

> Alexandra was referred to us because of examinations. Suddenly she was going to see a psychiatrist because of my referral. It jumped the waiting list because the things that I had heard from Alexandra were so scary. We have been told since day one that when people say that they want to commit suicide, we should take it seriously. Last year, I raised heaven and hell because I suddenly realised that Rose from Sonsa Primary was telling me that she wants to jump. She had said it to me two weeks before. And yet I realised that I should have

> told someone about this on the last day before I went abroad - I was frightened that something would happen while I was away and it would be my fault that I hadn't told anybody about this. So I asked someone for advice and they urged me to tell the mother to take the child to a psychiatrist. The person I asked for advice said "Can you imagine if this girl tries to jump off a high place and doesn't manage and then she's maimed for life - what would you tell the mother?" I thought it was a side-track; that it was beside the point. If I should refer to a psychiatrist, then I should refer to a psychiatrist - and that's that. If the referral is for the child's own good. But what if the referral is not for the child's own good? What happens if the result makes the child's life worse than it is - what happens if the child was coping, and because of my referral, then the child is suddenly a mental case - a child who takes medication - a child who is suicidal?
>
> Is this because I see people who go to a psychiatrist as stepping over the line from normal to abnormal? Is it because I see people who take medication for emotional difficulties as meaning they cannot cope with their emotions? I felt as strongly about this when my doctor once prescribed something to help me calm down and sleep. Suddenly I felt threatened with the label depression. I preferred to suffer the feelings - to find different ways of coping, than take medication, although I may have needed it. There's something different between needing medicine for a throat infection and taking medicine because you're feeling overwhelmed. But perhaps, taking medication for things like this doesn't mean you're hooked – you're not a nutter, or a mental case, a person seeing a psychiatrist, someone who doesn't have a locus of control which is more internal than external. If you think the psychiatrist is going to cure you, then you're never going to be cured - because you get dependent on the medication, etc.... (Journal: March, 2005).

When I visited the school a couple of weeks later, the assistant head told me that Alexandra seemed not herself and said that Alexandra was worried because, following my recommendation that she be seen by a doctor on account of her having frequent headaches, she was to have surgery to remove what was blocking her sinuses. It seemed that she had had an infection for a while and nobody had noticed – the only symptoms had been the daily headaches and bad breath. This was confirmed by Alexandra's mother when I called her and she said that they had only been told a day earlier that she would have to undergo surgery. Although she was already worried, I asked her whether Alexandra had spoken to her saying that we had made an agreement that she was to disclose something to her. She said that she had not and I proceeded to tell her that I was worried about her preoccupation with death. Although she agreed with this, further adding that part of her dislike for the operation was that she was afraid of dying during the procedure, she had not known the extent of her preoccupation.

I was not explicit about all the details which Alexandra had told me but I told her enough to worry her. I apologised for adding to her concerns but said that I had to let her know. I offered to refer Alexandra urgently to the hospital where a psychiatrist worked with a team of professionals and her mother agreed. I explained that we normally check such situations with a psychiatrist, that this was our procedure. She also said that she would take Alexandra to the counselling psychologist to whom they had all spoken in the hospital where her father had been cared for. So that was done – the mother took my concerns on board and was willing to take action.

But I was still not happy with myself or with the situation. I think I worried because of the sheer coincidence of how things had happened. If Alexandra had been referred to me because of her concerns and because she could not get over her grief for her father, I believe that I would not have got so worked up about the case. However, Alexandra had come to my notice because she was referred for exam concessions and it was directly through me that she might be needlessly pathologised.

> Why was I so ready to refer Alexandra? I had taken responsibility for myself and refused what the doctor had prescribed – but I had not been contemplating death as Alexandra had disclosed. I haven't passed through what Alexandra has been through, of course. Maybe she does need a little help, to get over this period. I referred Alexandra because it was procedure. I need to make sure that I am covered - that the responsibility is not mine - because I am not with her 24 hours a day - so I told the mother. And also because children who express thoughts of suicide are supposed to be seen by someone who understands psychopathology.
>
> But maybe, there isn't a line over which one steps into psychopathology. Maybe, one copes, and copes a little bit more, and then one needs help to continue coping, and then doesn't need more help in coping, and continues to cope. If only I could be sure that the psychiatrist shared this point of view - then I wouldn't worry anymore about how they will treat Alexandra when she goes in two days time. I hope that when they hear that she is seeing a counselling psychologist, this will prevent them from further pathologising her. Maybe I'm wrong about all this.
>
> But she was coping. She coped for 8 years with her father's illness. Was Alexandra really ready to burst or did I construct her as ready to burst? What will she think when she faces a psychiatrist in 2 days? There she was, opening her heart to me, and suddenly she's in a hospital, in the same group as some of the most unmanageable children we have ever seen. In one minute she was a child seen for SEAs and in another she was being referred to a psychiatrist. Was she always a child who should be referred to a psychiatrist, or did she become one because of my referral? The thing is - Alexandra may not have been suicidal - but she may become so now.
>
> What is the dilemma here? I acted according to procedure. The procedure is there for a reason, based on a history of cases and experienced professionals. But what about the individuality of Alexandra? So much is heard about distrusting psychiatrists and the medical model? What about the book on Deconstructing Psychopathology (Parker, et al., 1995) which I read? Can I apply it to this case? (Journal: January, 2005).

I called the mother to see how she was feeling about the imminent appointment. I felt I needed to speak to her – I believe I wanted to warn her, to ask her to be on her guard against possible pathologisation of her daughter. I think I wanted to make sure that the link between us was still there, so that I could still have some input on what happened after the hospital visit.

> I tried to give her the voice – but she doesn't have the language necessary – she doesn't have the knowledge and insight that goes with such language (Journal: January, 2005).

I was the professional, I was the one who knew the language, but Alexandra's mother did not. "Could it be that Alexandra and her mother do not possess language for the things they need and that I possess it and am saying it for them?" (Journal January 2005). When I tried to communicate to Alexandra's mother that I wanted her to be careful I did so by saying to her that I appreciated that she was her mother and that no one could tell her more about her daughter than she could herself. By diminishing my own power over her and Alexandra, I tried to empower. I did not think that she understood me however – she reiterated that we were the professionals and that we would be able to advise her. This may be a presumption on my part but at the time I recall thinking that it was wrong of me to think that I could 'give' her a voice, to 'empower' her.

> I didn't tell the mother about my thoughts. I kept them to myself - I didn't want to scare her.
>
> But by keeping my thoughts and dilemmas to myself, I may be acting in a morally incorrect way towards my clients - the mother and child. I didn't explain to the mother that I was afraid that Alexandra might be defined as pathological as a result of my referral. She took this step because I urged her to do so. I took this decision in my own hands. I decided for her - but my decision was based on the procedure, which was based on fear - fear of what would happen if something happened to Alexandra and the doctor had not been notified about her suspected state of mind. What are the power issues here? Did I have a right to refer Alexandra without going through these doubts with her? She wouldn't think of doubting in me, probably, as I am the psychologist. How am I using this power that I have as a professional?
>
> How would things have changed had I shared my doubts with her? Earlier I spoke about the fear of appearing woolly. Somehow I have to gain confidence about being woolly about things - I have to have confidence about being in a state of doubt. I have to trust that feeling unconfident might make me choose more ethical actions towards my clients. It is true that there is the risk that clients might lose confidence in you if you appear doubtful and not secure in your opinions. There is no easy answer to this. It would also not stand you in very good stead with your colleagues to appear unconfident. How to listen to their opinions and see their point and compare with your own and perhaps take on their own opinion in some cases but not in others?

It would appear very woolly. They would not see it as a good thing… (Journal: March, 2005).

5. THE AFTERMATH

The above was my dilemma, but, in all fairness, I need to continue to tell the story of what happened. I completed a referral form and tried to put in as much of the above issues as I could without having the reader of the form think that I was totally confused. I emphasised all the positive qualities which Alexandra had while explaining the difficulties which the family had passed through. Moreover, I explained my fears that she would be pathologised. Then I felt that I had done everything possible. While making sure that Alexandra's needs were seen to, I felt that I had done my best to prevent possible negative results. When I examined myself and my actions, I was satisfied that I could absolve myself of guilt and that, although many of my actions were also motivated by fear, still the end result should be positive mostly for Alexandra. But I was emotionally exhausted – were it not for the immense support which my partner gave me during this time, which also took the form of encouragement to write what I was going through, I do not know how I could have coped. The endless questions, the doubts and uncertainty, coupled with my own demons of insecurity and incompetence, had worn me out. It seemed as though I had made myself go through this, to purge myself of the wrongdoing which I suspected in myself in referring Alexandra.

I laughed at myself and at what I later called my histrionics when Alexandra's mother told me that the psychiatrist listened to Alexandra and recommended her to try to push these thoughts out of her head when they occurred to her. Alexandra was not even given another appointment. Her mother was just told to contact the hospital if she felt the necessity. While laughing at myself, I was still sober in reflecting about the story and my involvement in it. I had learnt so much about myself both personally and as a practitioner working in a system which has its own safety nets and loop holes. I was glad that I had experienced the fear and self doubt to the degree that I had – I feel that it sharpened my intuition and practitioner skills in preparation for what was to come. It was all right to be cautious and wary – it actually guaranteed that I was caring for Alexandra as a child, rather than as a case.

By the end of my involvement, Alexandra's mother phoned to thank me for my report because she had just heard from the smaller school which she had hoped her daughter would attend. She complimented me for my report "It shows that it was written by a professional…" We just kept reinforcing each other's roles of expert and non-expert, but I had learnt much from my involvement with that family.

By this time, I had decided to take Alexandra on as one of the cases which I would write about in my doctorate work. I had promised her and her mother that I would go one more time to see her before the holidays. A few months later, I went because of other referrals and asked to see her. She told me, "You didn't forget me, miss. You told me that you would come again and you did come!" How could I explain to her the amount of energy and work that I had already invested in her case, and that I was still planning to invest?

CHAPTER 10

PROFESSIONALISM AND PROCEDURE

> Within the last fifty years we have seen, within the UK, the rise of a predominantly professional society; the increase, that is, in the number of occupational groups claiming professional status. The tacit terms of the 1945 settlement were that professional autonomy would be granted in return for public service. Within this post 2nd World War era, the public sector professional, espousing the values of professional autonomy and the public service ethic, established a gold standard (Nixon, 2004, p. 29).

The sudden contrast between the end of the last chapter and the beginning of this one serves to highlight the sharp disparities between the considerations that the practitioner has to keep in mind in day to day work. While the story of Alexandra was taking place, a myriad other claims demanded my attention, many of which could not be dealt with using the same care which I was giving Alexandra and her mother. The differences in the requirements can be abrupt, so that the practitioner seems to have to switch certain aspects of his/her role on and off according to the necessity at hand. While the previous chapter focused primarily on Alexandra's story, this chapter, which links in with the previous, highlights the other claims on the practitioner's time and role. Issues of accountability and efficiency in professionalism are explored within the context of the recounted story. The professional autonomy mentioned in the above quotation is questioned considering the numerous checks and inspections which professionals nowadays go through. The chapter starts by mentioning some of the changes which society underwent in time, which changes resulted in an environment in which professionalism now flourishes. Although it may be a simplistic perspective, I am not claiming to present a historical point of view but want to emphasise the contrast, as seen by Durkheim (1984), between the set up of societies with different structures of solidarity, with the latter structure providing the context for professionalism to flourish, as seen by MacIntyre (2000), in terms of the self.

1. THE KIND OF SOCIETY WHICH NEEDS PROFESSIONALS

According to Durkheim, mechanical solidarity characterised societies in which division of labour did not yet feature. In such a society, the individual is linked directly to the group and the unity of the whole rules out individuality of the parts. The sole existing personality in such a society is the collective one as groups form in terms of ancestral relationships, and the source of ties in people living together is blood relationship. In this society, there is social solidarity arising from "a certain number of states of consciousness [which] are common to all members of the same society....The more varied the relationships on which that consciousness makes its action felt, the more also it creates ties that bind the individual to the group; the more, consequently, social cohesion derives entirely from this cause and bears this imprint" (1984, p. 64). What one does in such a society is not as important as who one is and where one belongs to. Status is not achieved but ascribed.

> I am brother, cousin and grandson, member of this household, that village, this tribe. These are not characteristics that belong to human beings accidentally, to be stripped away in order to discover 'the real me'. They are part of my substance, defining partially at least and sometimes wholly my obligations and my duties. Individuals inherit a particular space within an interlocking set of social relationships; lacking that space, they are nobody, or at best a stranger or an outcast (MacIntyre, 2000, p. 33–34).

Durkheim calls this solidarity mechanical as he likens it to an inorganic body, whose molecules lack any movement of their own owing to the cohesion that links them together. "The individual consciousness, considered from this viewpoint, is simply a dependency of the collective type, and follows all its motions just as the object possessed follows those which its owner imposes upon it. In societies where this solidarity is highly developed the individual…does not belong to himself; he is literally a thing at the disposal of society" (1984, p. 84).

The solidarity in which the professions and professionalism flourished was characterised by a division of labour. This kind of solidarity does not see individuals resembling one another but assumes that they are different from one another. The individuality of the whole grows at the same time as that of the parts, but "the greater the unity of the organism, the more marked the individualisation of the parts" (Durkheim, 1984, p. 85); thus Durkheim calls this solidarity 'organic'. Society is here likened to a body made up of various organs, each of which depends on the other and on the whole. Each organ has a special role and is itself formed from differentiated parts. This mutual dependence signifies that while specialising more in what each organ does, there is, however, a complete reliance on the function of other organs, without which one organ cannot survive. When writing about division of labour, Adam Smith (1776) explains: "This great increase of the quantity of work which, in consequence of the division of labour, the same number of people are capable of performing, is owing to three different circumstances; first, to the increase of dexterity in every particular workman; secondly, to the saving of the time which is commonly lost in passing from one species of work to another; and lastly, to the invention of a great number of machines which facilitate and abridge labour, and enable one man to do the work of many" [internet source].

Individuals in this kind of Durkheim's solidarity are distributed within it according to the specific nature of their social activity. Their profession constitutes their "natural and necessary environment" (1984, p. 132) and the position of each individual is determined by the function which she fulfils. MacIntyre (2000) writes that the self is now criterionless, as no longer having any social identity "because the kind of *telos* in terms of which it once judged and acted is no longer thought to be credible" (p. 33). Thus, Durkheim's old mechanical solidarity frame cannot continue to host this new ever-increasing system and "this is why it must disappear" (1984, p. 133). There is no longer a collective consciousness and the segments are only united by their dependence on one another. As MacIntyre (2000) claims, in becoming free from the social bonds of premodern society, the modern self has lost its traditional boundaries provided by a social identity and also a perspective of life as having a purpose. Durkheim, in the second half of the nineteenth century, was already foreseeing that "the day will come when the whole of our social and political organisation will have an exclusively, or almost exclusively, professional basis" (Durkheim, 1984, p. 139).

Nixon mentions the post-war settlement "which had granted the professions status and authority on the basis of their expert knowledge" (Nixon et al., 1997, p. 5). He writes that new relationships between professionals and the public they serve have to be built in order for professionals to re-establish their power base. When writing about academic professionalism, Nixon (2001c) says that it is difficult to speak of academic workers as a unified profession. Stratification meant increased and deepening divisions of labour, leading to workers becoming increasingly isolated, but, as Durkheim (1984) described in his model of organic solidarity, Nixon says that these workers have also had to become increasingly accountable. The latter is an example, as Durkheim mentioned, of what unifies the organism.

2. PROCEDURE AND POLICY – ACCOUNTABILITY

Today's society, according to Nixon (2003), is ever more characterised by "accelerating individualisation", which makes us experience the world as 'runaway', a metaphor taken from Beck and BeckGernsheim (2002, in Nixon 2003). Owing to the increase in difference and change, what is at the foundation of institutions is no longer the assumption of homogeneity, this being, according to Nixon, about the notions of commonality and sameness. Institutions are now deemed as 'good' if they are able to cope with difference and change, thus putting heterogeneity as a characteristic worth cultivating. In this, institutions are reflecting the 'runaway world', already described in Chapter 3.

In this kind of world, it is very difficult to continue to compartmentalise and classify reality and we are thus growing more and more aware that what we thought was neat and controllable was in fact an illusion. Professionals, who were accustomed to being regarded as experts (Schön, 2000), have had to acknowledge that "things are complex, diffuse and messy" (Law, 2006). Schön tells about the crisis of confidence in professional knowledge, even among the professionals themselves, and that "scientists and scientifically trained professionals found themselves in the unfamiliar role of villain" (2000, p. 10). No longer can professionals claim the monopoly of knowledge and social control. This crisis of confidence also extends, I believe, to the area of education, social work, psychology and other helping professions. In an attempt to streamline practice, a system of checks and inspections has been adopted to safeguard members of society.

People can get lost in cracks in the system in a society where we have grown accustomed to have services. "Indeed, on the one hand, each of us depends more intimately upon society the more labour is divided up, and on the other, the activity of each one of us, is correspondingly more specialised, the more personal it is" (Durkheim, 1984, p. 85). Thus, in our society we have had to make do with this by ensuring that everybody is accounted for, that it is made very clear which roles are whose and where accountability stops. We need to know whom it is we can blame when something goes wrong. And the fear that something *might* go wrong drives our every action. Professions are regulated, templates and proformas are issued, schools and services are inspected, even risks are assessed (an oxymoron if there ever was one). Any issue or situation is categorised and operationalised, into doable actions. It is as though professionals are not trusted to do their job to the best of their abilities anymore, and so it is made sure that they do so in a very forceful way. What then happens, however, is that the professional ceases to be a professional but merely follows the prescribed actions of his/her work *because* they are prescribed. It seems to be forgotten that such actions, even such attitudes, originally went with the job. The motivation, the vocation and good will of professionals is missed out, because they are listed in a check-list with many tick-boxes beside each item.

MacIntyre (2000) addresses this point when he makes the difference between acting from duty and acting from inclination while exploring the virtues of acknowledged dependence. His view is that although a person might not have the inclination to do what s/he ought to do, that person would have learnt that it must be done out of duty. "Do we then perhaps sometimes act from duty when we ought instead to act from inclination? Yes, replies Hume, we do so when we have recognised in ourselves the lack of some requisite motive: 'a person who feels his heart devoid of that motive, may hate himself upon that account, and may perform the action without the motive, from a certain sense of duty, in order to acquire by practice that virtuous principle, or at least, to disguise to himself, as much as possible, his want of it' (p. 479)" (Hume in MacIntyre, 2000, p. 122). And yet, we are driven by the fear that professionals will not act out of such motivation.

Society thus objectifies, institutionalises and operationalises what professionals ought to do out of inclination or duty, to ensure that one way or another, it is being done. The sad consequence of this is that the reason for the necessary actions being done changes. People do what they have to do because they are going to be checked, because they are going to be held accountable, because otherwise there will be sanctions. What is driving them is external – that which is internal, which is always less respected (particularly as it cannot be quantified) and less nurtured, is being lost. Ironically, these targets, standards and levels are all attempts to ensure that the judgement of professionals is sound. However, "any attempt to limit the complexity of professional intervention would, from the perspective I am here outlining, only result in de-professionalisation – in the restriction of the role of professional practitioner to that of the technical operative" (Nixon, 2004a, p. 33). It is also rendering the institutions in which professionals work, as well as the professionals themselves, "defensive and inward-looking: 'we are heading towards defensive medicine, defensive teaching and defensive policing' (O'Neill, 2002, p. 50)" (Nixon, 2003, p. 8). There is a great mis-targeting of energy which rises from fear. This very much ties up with my involvement with Alexandra. My decision to follow the procedure and refer Alexandra, notwithstanding my reluctance to pathologise what I believed was part of her grieving process, was mainly based on fear and was a defensive action on my part.

3. PROCEDURE AND POLICY – EFFICIENCY

Besides the ever increasing need for accountability in the institutions in which we live and work today, there is also great emphasis on efficiency. This further confirms Nixon's comparison of the practitioner to the technical operative. Lyotard (1979) says that technology follows the principle of optimal performance, which is that of maximising output and minimising input. "Technology is therefore a game pertaining not to the true, the just, or the beautiful, etc., but to efficiency: a technical 'move' is 'good' when it does better and/or expends less energy than another" [internet source].

As is the story in many places of work in the caring professions, at my place of work there are scarce resources in the face of a rather large work load. As a result of working in such a situation, I feel demoralised and defeated. Whatever fight there once was in me, sometimes seems to be all gone, and a learned helplessness replaces it. I am motivated in my work with individual children and parents and enjoy the relationships with them, but feel helpless and demotivated in the general picture. I feel that I am becoming deskilled because of the pressures of my job and remember longingly the time when I used to think that in-service training, creating circles of friends for children and other projects were part of my job description.

Although I try to keep myself on my toes, also through my reading and writing, I find that when decisions are taken for me I feel comfortable as I have less to worry about. As I worry about how I am to meet the deadlines and reduce the case load, there is less space for me to worry about some of the decisions which go with my profession. If there are guidelines, I feel that I am relieved from responsibility and do not need to reach my own decision. I am not accountable for my actions if I am following guidelines. Guidelines, procedures and policies also help in that if something unpleasant has to be done, I find it easier to blame "them" for my unpleasant act and "their" anonymity further reduces accountability.

However, in so doing, I am risking losing that fine sense which I need to know what is just and what is unjust, that moral purposiveness which Nixon (2004a) mentions, and also the mental state of trying to change something which ought not to be. My work is not only an individualistic endeavour, but takes place in a social and "indeed often highly politicised context" (2004a, p. 30). The moral considerations of my occupation need to be acknowledged as a prerequisite of being professional – I cannot be an educational psychologist without being a moral educational psychologist. The ends and purposes of my professional judgement are, or ought to be, morally purposeful, in that they "prefigure a better, or at least more decent, society" (Nixon, 2004a, p. 31). I need to make sure that I keep that fine sense sharp. The regulating professional bodies try to ensure that this takes place by requiring registered practitioners to have regular supervision and a certain amount of Continuous Professional Development as a prerequisite for keeping that registration which professionals covet. Everything is done so that the best possible level of professionalism is maintained. And yet, this jars with the aforementioned preoccupation with efficiency:

> It scarcely needs saying that the preoccupation with efficiency and effectiveness, with performativity, is ... a malaise with deep causes in the totalising ways of thinking.... The vocabulary of ... policy and practice also – makes it

> difficult, if not impossible, to think differently about these matters (Standish, 2001, p. 514).

4. GOING THROUGH THE MOTIONS

However, if I do go through the motions specified by the regulating professional bodies, will that guarantee that I have moral purposiveness in my work? Is that not another check-list with tick boxes? Morality and ethics are always present in our professional lives, and do not just come into effect at points of conflict, or what are known as moral dilemmas (Standish, 2001, 2002c). I already explained in the introduction that we are constantly faced with non-situations which are so because there does not seem to be a point of decision, as one would expect. I still call these dilemmas because of their complex and confusing nature and also because even after the moment passes, one is still left feeling confused and unsure of whether the right thing was done. The action not followed, moreover, still continues to make itself felt through the action which was taken – it keeps it in place. The actions not followed are almost ghostly in nature – they appear and disappear when one is not expecting them (Derrida, 1992).

In the story of my involvement with Alexandra, there were a number of issues which I had decided to problematise rather than to take the comfortable stance. Rather than limiting my discussion with her mother to Alexandra's schooling, I decided to pay attention to the whole story which this woman had to tell. This led to my deciding that my involvement in Alexandra's case could not only be on the grounds of the special examination arrangements (SEA) which were the original reason for referral. I had a discussion here with some of my colleagues during a meeting on whether we should treat SEA cases as 'normal' cases or not. I decided to prefer to dedicate more energy and 'do a better job' on fewer referrals, than to see more children. This was seen as unjust by some colleagues who pressed the claim of the other children on our service. I think that here I was also thinking about myself, in that I wanted to do something which I felt worthwhile, and not just try to 'service' all children, losing myself in the process. This is another situation where Nagel's (2002) five sources of value mentioned in Chapter 8 can be seen. Which one of us was right in our arguments? I was giving importance to my obligation to Alexandra and her mother, and also wanted to have the satisfaction that I was making a good and complete job of it. These correspond to the first, fourth and fifth of Nagel's fundamental types. The arguments of those colleagues who urged the claims of other children were also giving value to Nagel's first and corresponded also to the second and third source of value. They were thinking that Alexandra ought not be given what might be termed as preferential treatment, especially as other children may be put at a disadvantage by my decision. How to give priority to the values which above arguments are using?

I do not claim that the ways which I chose are right and that the alternative options were wrong. What I am saying is that it is very important that these questions are raised in the first place. It is too easy to feel that one is doing what one can, without problematising one's actions. In his article on the sense of the given in research,

Standish (2001) urges us to make the given strange by more rigorous examination of "what it is to take something as given, and from where the given or the gift comes" (p. 505). I use his idea to urge that we practitioners make our accepted values and routines strange by constantly putting them to question and to prevent ourselves from becoming complacent. Standish quotes Heidegger and says that "We need to be goaded to prevent us from subsiding into a way of thinking that 'carries an air of harmlessness and ease, which causes us to pass lightly over what really deserves to be questioned' (Heidegger, 1968, p. 154)" (Standish, 2001, p. 502). In this way we lightly say that we have to cater for two hundred applications for Special Examination Arrangements while at the same time saying that we want to do a good job. It may seem that there is a comfortable union between the two ideas and that they are neutral. But it is not neutral, and not comfortable – it is problematic. The problem is always time. Blake et al. (1998, p. 1) start their very interesting book by quoting Lyotard who writes that thinking wastes time in a world that identifies success with saving time. The authors' book is entitled 'Thinking again', which "will be to waste time twice over, unless the presuppositions of the modern world are themselves faulty" (Blake et al., 1998, p. 1). The authors further promise us that their book will not save us time.

What Standish (2001) recommends in research I would like to apply in my practice: the need to hold at arm's length what is already known to avoid preconceptions, as these prevent one from gaining the larger view. Standish follows T.S. Eliot's (1986) advice here, which is to go by a way which is the way of ignorance in order to arrive at what one does not know.

The trusted and tried methods of practice, then, should be suspect, should be 'thought again'. It is possible for one to go through the motions of becoming an educational psychologist but this same person may be blinded by her preconceptions unless steps are taken to ensure otherwise. Numerous standards and checks are put in place in order to ensure that society gets the helping professionals which are required. This may be unsatisfactory on two counts. Primarily, it might happen that a person could go through the motions of a trainee and might eventually reach that professional target but may not have the right aptitude or attitude for it. My issue is that all these check ups and qualifications are aimed at guaranteeing something which they do not necessarily guarantee – at the end of the day there is still nothing which guarantees good practice in the more abstract sense. We try to bring it down to the nitty-gritty – but you cannot pin down real good practice.

On the other hand, these very standards and checks which are meant to ensure good practice may, by their very nature be stifling good practice, because by listing the exact motions which a good practitioner is meant to do, they might actually be choking that which originally used to spur people to doing such things. This is, in fact, what McAuliffe and Sudbury (2005) conclude in their study which found that the organisational supervision ostensibly established to ensure standards and ethical practice was the least satisfactory space for staff to reflect on such situations: "Many policies introduced for apparently rational and laudable purposes have unintended negative consequences, and it may well be that organisational emphasis on performance management, procedural monitoring, and staff control have the effect of minimising effective attention to critical aspects of effective and ethical service" (McAuliffe and Sudbury, 2005, p. 39). The helping professions did not always exist – some persons may have been more caring and have more understanding than others and by time, this quality in a person, this attitude, became a role and eventually a profession. As Nixon (2004a) says, "thoughtfulness is ordinary… [It] is a common resource" (p. 32). So when professionals are being thoughtful they "are doing something that is not categorically different from what human beings generally are doing when they are thinking through their pain, their aspirations, their dilemmas, their hurts, their personal histories, etc" (ibid.).

We have turned the table upside down because rather than checking whether persons have this caring and understanding quality *before* they enter the profession, we try to regulate them *after* they have done so. In doing so, we are almost defeating the purpose. It almost offends me that I have procedures and policies to follow – I do not need a policy to make sure that I do my work to the utmost of my abilities. It then turns out that my good work, rather than caused by my own intention, is seen as a response to a policy. I am not being arrogant here – but I am expressing indignation as it seems as though I am not being trusted to feel, to think, to act in the right way, which is the way calculated to best help the client. It seems that 'society' believes that I need these guidelines, otherwise goodness knows what I might do. "What is clear is that sometime in the end of the 20th Century the public service became estranged from the notion of professionalism and that the trade-off between the public service ethic and professional autonomy gave way to bureaucratic accountability." (Nixon, 2004a, p. 29). Predictability and safety-nets take the place of creativity and initiative. They may be there in an attempt to make things easier for the professionals, while others might maintain that they are another way of regulating our movements, something which we may have to resist. But "professional intervention is always complex, in the sense of being reliant upon modes of thought that take seriously the reality of human contingency and the unpredictability of human action" (Nixon, 2004a, p. 33).

In the attempt to streamline, then, we are willing to sacrifice individual style, and indeed, individual morality. Is it because we are afraid that the morality of the individuals who are professionals might not be the kind that we like? Again, is this a question of regulation, or is it that we do not trust each other? Is it because society and life in general are so fast that they want to make it easier for us to work, or to think? Why are we so frightened of leaving any room for uncertainty and dilemmas – are we becoming so unforgiving? Cannot we be trusted to do the best we can for the people we work with? Is it not obvious anymore that those persons who want to have this kind of job, such as an educational psychologist, must have these qualities, these values, these thoughts? It seems as though we are being told that we do not need to have values, because these will be provided in the policies which have been made for us. Nixon mentions the moral concerns which the caring professions share to be "the virtues of truthfulness (accuracy, sincerity), the virtues of respect (attentiveness, honesty) and the virtues of authenticity (courage, compassion)" (2004a, p. 31). These are very serious questions, I feel, because if we cannot be trusted ethically, then are we really worthy of the name professionals? "Without that ethical content our various professional occupations become devoid of their professionalism" (p. 31).

It is very important to think very hard and critically about how the helping professions are letting the pressures of a fast and demanding society shape their development, not to use the word degeneration. If training courses focus more on the content at the expense of the skills and moral dimensions of professional practice, this situation will continue to deteriorate. The centre of attention needs to consist once again of the search for a sense of moral purposefulness and less on the emphasis on performativity and target outcomes which bureaucratic accountability measures. We need to continue to struggle to do things thoughtfully, because that is what makes us professionals.

5. DIFFERENT SLANTS IN VARIOUS PROFESSIONAL TRAINING COURSES

When I was a trainee educational psychologist, the professional training course was being examined by persons sent from the regulating professional body to ensure that the course was still worthy of being accredited and recognised by this institution. Throughout this whole day, these persons spoke to our tutors, saw various papers and even met with us trainees. Prior to our meeting with them, we discussed the event among ourselves and I remember being particularly struck by a remark passed by one of the other trainees: she said that we ought to be careful about what we criticised because if it turned out that our course was not very good and if word got out that our course was not very good, how would that reflect on us as soon-to-be newly-qualified educational psychologists? Nonetheless, she was one of the few to criticise the course heavily, so much so, that I felt it incumbent on me to speak to one of the inspectors following the interview to say that her views by no means reflected the views of all the trainees in the course.

The training course we followed professed to be based on a learning model in which the trainees were expected to take decisions about where the individual lacunae of knowledge were. Our tutors were at hand to help us individually, as well as as a group, to fill these lacunae. The professional course was not set up with the aim of providing us with all the knowledge that a trainee educational psychologist was expected to have. It assumed that we were not all starting at the same point, but that each one of us had strengths through previous study and work experience. In the beginning of the training, we were rather disappointed and thought that we had entered the wrong course. This came to a head when we met trainees from different training courses.

The trainees from other universities seemed to agree in their views about their respective courses whereas we felt particularly bad about ours at that time, and yet none of us really wanted to appear at a disadvantage in front of future colleagues. We would be meeting these other trainees in jobs following our training and we did not want to have our already fragile confidence undermined. When they spoke about their course, they moaned about the huge amount of handouts and notes which they were constantly given about each and every condition which we might meet in children. They were even taught problem-solving methods, just like doctors and vets are taught in their assessment procedures. One particular group of trainees mentioned the joke which they had about trees in Scandinavian forests being felled because of the educational psychology training course due to the large amount of paper handed out throughout the course.

We felt angry and peeved at our course organisers, who did not give us as many handouts and did not arm us with problem-solving techniques which were proven to work, but at the same time we were also confused and doubtful. It had not yet dawned on us that our course consisted more of personal formation and on our gaining a questioning attitude in search of understanding, rather than on knowledge acquisition. Our training course was aimed more towards forming its trainees and arming them with skills. Although we still wanted to have answers to basic questions, such as 'how can I help a child with dyslexia?' or 'what are the characteristics of children with autism?', our course tried to prepare us for the real-life cases, where children's difficulties were very rarely as clear-cut as that. "Professional judgement … comes into play at precisely those points where common sense guidelines are unclear and the criteria open to multiple interpretation.… Professional judgement is a risky and unpredictable business" (Nixon, 2004a, p. 30). As Schön (2000) mentioned, "we have become aware of the importance to actual practice of phenomena – complexity, uncertainty, instability, uniqueness, and value-conflict – which do not fit the model of Technical Rationality" (p. 39). I am by no means denigrating the training which other trainees had – I am simply appreciating my own training and explaining why I found it difficult to do so earlier.

The problem is, I believe, that we feel comfortable with means-end reasoning, but in following such reasoning we subjugate our profession to procedural criteria which is in the nature of our profession to avoid. There is a "rise in instrumental reasoning and a growing preoccupation with procedure over substance or content" (Standish, 2002, p. 6). Richard Smith goes to Francis Bacon for the origin of such reasoning and quotes his belief that "the mind itself be from the very outset not left to take its own course, but guided at every step, and the business be done as if by machinery" (Ellis and Spedding (trans.) in Robertson, 1905, in Smith, 2006, p. 157). Technique, rather than talent is what is important and thus, "the essential thing…is to possess a method" (p. 158). Smith quotes Appleyard (1992, p. 51) saying that "the Baconian gets on with the job", but however insists that, notwithstanding the clarity and simplicity of the rules outlined, "sooner or later, and probably sooner rather than later, judgement must be applied" (Smith, 2006, p. 159). This puts the rub in Bacon's belief that almost anyone can use his new method. Judgement is not a question of pronouncing that 1 + 1 = 2, but "requires the tacit or personal knowledge of whoever is making the judgement" (Nixon, 2004a, p. 30). As Law points out, "while standard methods are often extremely good at what they do, they are badly adapted to the study of the ephemeral, the indefinite and the irregular" (2006, p. 4), while I insist that there is nothing in our work to which these three adjectives would be inappropriately applied. This is the reason for which I reiterate that when, as professionals, we feel our 'methods' becoming standard, that is when we have to be alarmed.

CONCLUSION

In concluding this chapter, the following is introduced, as it ends with a quotation from MacIntyre (2000) who emphasises that practice is not just a set of technical skills, but is more than the totality of such skills because it contributes to human flourishing:

> …a practice, in the sense intended, is never just a set of technical skills, even when directed towards some unified purpose and even if the exercise of those skills can on occasion be valued or enjoyed for their own sake. What is distinctive in a practice is in part the way in which conceptions of the relevant goods and ends which the technical skills serve – and every practice does require the exercise of technical skills – are transformed and enriched by these extensions of human powers and by that regard for its own internal goods which are partially definitive of each particular practice or type of practice (p. 193).

CHAPTER 11

PROFESSIONALISM AND JUDGEMENT

INTRODUCTION

This chapter starts by drawing together the various threads which have been weaved in this book so that a leaning towards a conclusion may be assayed. Following an outline of the points on which the book was structured, a discussion about practical judgement suggests that virtues may be what allow practitioners to work in difficult settings, asking the questions put forward in this book. What then ensues is the political and ethical aspect, that is, how the above can be seen in the profession of educational psychology. As had been made clear in Chapter 1, although a number of narratives from professional practice were used to put the theory in context, questions are asked in the larger picture, beyond the individual practitioner, questions which have been relevant to various helping professions working with children and families.

1. PULLING THREADS TOGETHER

A psychoanalytic note was heard throughout which highlighted the urge of every person to move towards stability. Klein's writing on the process of splitting provided the context of the self which is non-unitary, which point is adopted by Hollway's (1994) research that does not see the subjectivity of research participants as rational and unitary. Instead the possibility of conflicting views and emotions are permissible within her research framework. This is also put forward by Billig et al.'s (1988) research, which explains that it is possible that one person can have two conflicting answers for the same item in a questionnaire. Billig emphasises that everyday life is shaped by dilemmatic qualities so that confused thoughts within persons are more common than is allowed in traditional research.

However, persons still strive for the balance so that stability may be achieved. The search for balance is ethical in nature, as the argument is put forward that everything one does has ethical implications (Standish, 2001, 2002c). Stability is reached, only to be upset again with new input which eventually is worked into a new stability. The notion that the practitioner is in a constant state of becoming is thus introduced. This may contrast with the idea of the practitioner as one who deals in facts, who has arrived at a destination. This differs from the omniscient practitioner who knows and who has certainty about the practice about which she is an expert. The practitioner who is constantly becoming allows herself to be uncertain. Webster and Lunt (2002) quote Eraut (1994) who defines professional conduct as "wise judgement under conditions of uncertainty" (p. 102). Rather than suppressing uncertainty and the fear which accompanies such a state through the frantic search for certainty, the practitioner learns to live with uncertainty and turns it to the advantage of the children and persons she works with. In so doing, while the practitioner still looks to increase her knowledge and skills, there is nonetheless awareness that these do not in themselves provide answers to the difficulties which clients present. Practising with uncertainty allows for the client to present issues which do not fit, without the sceptical almost desperate search on the part of the practitioner to see where such a client may be compartmentalised.

Tolerating not knowing therefore allows the practitioner to use practical judgement which always places the client's welfare first and foremost. Damasio (1999) claims that consciousness must be present so that the feelings which a person experiences can influence beyond the here and now. Thus, when the practitioner accepts and understands uncertainty and the fear which normally accompanies it, there is a move from the kind of reasoning which the Greeks called *techne*, towards *phronesis*, which is a form of reasoning "acquired by practitioners who, in seeking to achieve the standards of excellence inherent in their practice, develop the capacity to make wise and prudent judgements about what, in a particular situation, would constitute an appropriate expression of the good" (Carr, 2006, p. 426). Explanation of the above in greater detail will follow. Bion (1994) writes that meaning is obtained through experience and calls for the suspension of memory and desire so that a stop can be put to the suppression of uncertainty. The links between the experiences which the practitioner has will provide meaning and understanding as the undigested sensory experiences (beta elements, as explained in Chapter 6) are converted through the alpha function into alpha elements. Thus the practitioner comes to tolerate what was previously indigestible and can gain understanding.

I argue that if the practitioner allows her personal self to participate in the professional self, contrary themes and uncertainty may be seen as less of a threat. The 'runaway' world in which practice takes place is fraught with dilemmas and the way that psychology may try to deal with the complexity which is people is to have an excessive concern with hygiene (taken from Law's views on research, 2006), thus seeming to be very removed from reality. Law urges us to stop seeking to acquire certainty, to arrive at stable conclusions and to believe that we have the ability to have special insights – we need to unmake the desire for security. Through this, the practitioner will be better equipped to make those judgements in her work, because she will have an awareness of the implications for clients and also because she ceases to have merely a technical role but takes on a more professional role, thus combining uncertainty with moral purposefulness and making more space for the ethical in everyday practice.

2. PROCEDURE AND POLICY - JUDGEMENT

It has been established that a practitioner may frequently find herself in a situation in which the next step cannot easily be seen. In such situations, I find myself asking for colleagues' thoughts and we discuss cases and think about reasons for which we feel strongly against one course of action or another. In Alexandra's story, this meant that I was considering the possibility of not referring Alexandra for psychiatric assessment as I did not want to pathologise her grief. But I had been taught that the procedure was so – and required such and such an action from the practitioner. My fear was that the procedure, this time, was not going to help but was going to harm Alexandra.

> Professional accounts…cannot be separated from the wider cultural context... [Representations] affect the categories of behaviour which are considered pathological, removing them from being understood in relation to the broader social context. Secondly, they affect the interpretation of behaviour…Thirdly they affect the kinds of interventions offered… (Parker, et al., 1995, p. 65).

It would be fairly easy to ensure that practitioners know the procedures and policies before they enter a place of work. If necessary, an examination could be carried out to assess the extent of practitioners' knowledge of such matters. However, what cannot be made certain is whether a practitioner knows how she is to apply what the procedure says in particular situations - this ability is what makes a professional use practical reasoning (judgement), as opposed to technical reasoning which operates in terms of means-end. Can a practitioner take the spirit of a policy and try to follow that, instead of following the print with which the spirit of the policy is laid out? If a practitioner were to make her own judgement about the contingencies of a situation involving a child and thus act in that child's best interests, surely the practitioner in question is not at fault but is living up to the requirement of the profession. Circumstances change situations somewhat and it is essential that a practitioner appraises a situation and makes a decision about what is to be done. However, what should be remembered is that a policy or procedure is there for the very specific purpose of preventing particular circumstances from interfering in the prescribed courses of action. A practitioner working in a service is expected to follow that prescribed course.

On the other hand, being a professional means that one is trusted to work for the well-being of the children or families receiving the service of the professional. It is very important to address the possibility of the practitioner deciding against following prescribed courses in the training of such professionals. The judgement of the professional can be seen as that which particularly distinguishes her from the non-professional. "The claim of any occupational group to professional status is based upon its capacity to make informed and authoritative judgements regarding the adequacy of available evidence, the provenance of that evidence, and the options available in the light of that evidence. Judgement is paramount" (Nixon, 2004a, p. 30). I recall once being told to ensure that my recommendations fall within the set procedures. Could it be that a professional is told to follow policy and procedure to such an extent that she feels that her professionalism is being undermined? Is there not the constant danger of the professional becoming de-skilled? It often crosses my mind as I sit at my desk in the service where I work that I am becoming a pen-pusher, in the worst sense of the word. Not only do I move from one bit of writing to another with monotonous heaviness, but what is worse, I also feel that I am getting accustomed to it and feel myself sliding to a comfortable sensation where the *uncomfortable* feeling of never having done enough subsides and recedes. That uncomfortable feeling was what used to keep me on my toes, sometimes over-anxious and fearful, but I felt vibrant and alive to situations which surrounded me. In such situations I work with facts, with certainty and without contingency.

When explaining professional judgement, Nixon (2004a) terms it as being a risky and unpredictable business and as having a complex and indeterminate nature. "Judgements do not come ready made: they cannot simply be read off from evidence. They require the tacit or personal knowledge of whoever is making the judgement. The notion of wisdom is often attached to judgement precisely because it makes this necessary connection between the evidence upon which judgement is based and the tacit knowledge which the professional brings to bear upon that evidence" (ibid., p. 30). As mentioned in the previous chapter, judgement is not a matter of simple routine, unless of course, the professional wants to question that simplicity. Professional judgement "comes into play at precisely those points where common sense guidelines are unclear and the criteria open to multiple interpretation" (Nixon ibid.). While agreeing with Nixon here, I would like to add another caveat: I argue that judgement is also exercised when the common sense guidelines are apparently clear. In professional practice we ought to constantly question even whether we are being duped (perhaps even by ourselves) into thinking that matters are straightforward and thus might be taking things for granted which we ought to problematise. These are ways in which practitioners can prevent themselves from relying only on technical means-end reasoning. "The supposition that technical skills alone are enough to deliver client requirements simply neglects the ethical relationship in which those requirements are brought to light" (Hinchliffe, 2004, p. 546).

Thus, as Hinchliffe (2004) points out, there is an ethical factor to professional judgement which cannot be replaced. Standish would say, and I would agree with him, that the ethical is not just a factor, but is what holds the professional judgement together. Perhaps the point is that to deny or ignore the ethical would be to be unprofessional. "Professional judgement is … morally purposeful. ...To be professional is to acknowledge the moral dimension of one's occupation: to recognise that one has a moral career as well as just a career" (Nixon, 2004a, p. 31). When one is morally purposeful, there is a different feel to it when compared to the following of ethical codes, policies and prescribed procedures of action. As the latter are put down black on white, they seem to be closed, as though the discussion regarding their content is ended. On the other hand, being morally purposeful means that one is engaging with a never-ending process, the debate is still open and we are not sure about the boundaries of such a process. This is Nixon's (2004c) reconciliation of uncertainty with purposefulness. This is also the way in which Small (2001) talks about codes of ethics and about the role of philosophy in their development: "…a code is a finished product, whereas philosophy is a continuing process" (p. 392). Although Small is referring to codes of ethics in the research process, his argument can be applied to the role of the practitioner. A document, such as a policy, is institutionalised at a given time and practitioners are not expected to dialogue with it, but to comply with what it says "and sometimes there are penalties attached to failure to comply" (p. 392). Nixon (2004c) also emphasises the ongoing exercise of deliberation of moral purposefulness, which "is not a rationally pre-specified end-point which we then devise the technical means of attaining" (p. 120). The question is, then, what kind of practitioners is required to ensure that practical judgement is exercised in practice? How can one ask from practitioners that they can practise in toleration of uncertainty? How can practitioners, who would have struggled in their training and studies, be taught that rather than being experts and dealing in facts, they are in a constant process of becoming?

3. GOODNESS LIES IN PRACTICE

This section attempts to address what has been hinted at throughout the book, that is, that practitioners need virtues in order to practise. What should be emphasised at the start of this section is that there seems to be no clear distinction between the practice of work and the practice of life, and that in order to flourish, one should constantly attempt to reach the flourishing. This will be explained further below.

I would like to start by explaining what virtues are and how they can influence practice. As Nixon maintains, the virtuous life "can only be constructed through the living of it" (2004c, p. 117). Jordan and Meara (1990) make a distinction between virtue ethics and principle ethics, where the former focuses on character development which provides the basis for professional judgement, and the latter centres on acts and choices. Whereas those mostly using principle ethics ask the question "What shall I do?", in virtue ethics, the question asked is "Who shall I be?"

> The emphasis [is] not so much on actions as on agents and not so much on principles for deciding as on virtues for living. It is not as if principles are unimportant; rather, they are simply not enough. Whereas principles reflect guides for decision and action, rules, and codes of conduct, virtues reflect the internal composition of character (Jordan and Meara, 1990, p. 109).

MacIntyre draws upon the virtues as explained in Aristotle's *Nicomachean Ethics*. According to MacIntyre, "a good is something which we judge to be worthwhile to have, achieve, attend to, or participate in" (Higgins, 2003 p. 280), and thus is the reason for our actions. It is the goal of an action, known as the *telos*. It is important, however, that we desire the good because it is good, and pursue it not because it will give us satisfaction, but because we value it for its own sake besides for the fact that it contributes to our flourishing. We achieve the good through the virtues, but we must be able to appreciate the virtues for their own sake before they can be useful for us to help us achieve the good. This, according to MacIntyre (2000), can be encountered in practice. Many papers that I have read have quoted MacIntyre's definition of a practice (eg: Katayama, 2003; Higgins, 2003). I believe that this is mostly because the author uses such long and complicated sentences that he is impossible to paraphrase while retaining the same nuances which he intended:

> By a practice I am going to mean any coherent and complex form of socially established cooperative human activity through which the goods internal to that form of activity are realised in the course of trying to achieve those standards of excellence which are appropriate to, and partially definitive of, that form of activity, with the result that human powers to achieve excellence, and

> human conceptions of the ends and goods involved, are systematically extended (MacIntyre, 2000, p. 187).

According to MacIntyre's definition, the helping professions would not be seen as a practice, just like he believes that teaching is not. "What I have said implies that teaching itself is not a practice, but a set of skills and habits put to the service of a variety of practices" (MacIntyre and Dunne, 2002, p. 5). If this idea is followed, that would be, as Dunne (2003) said, an underestimation (p. 368) and also an impoverished view (p. 357) of our work. The helping professional does not go into a situation where she is referred and put her tools into use without all the judgements necessary to taking such a decision, keeping in mind the difficulties of taking decisions as mentioned in Chapter 3. Dunne (2003) accuses MacIntyre of having an "exclusive emphasis on the structure of the practice" which neglects "the complexity of the teaching situation, the fluctuating forces at work in it, and hence the dynamic character of what it puts in play between teacher and students. There is always something at stake for the teacher and the students, so that success – defined largely by the goods of the subject but conditioned by the complexities of the situation – is never guaranteed" (Dunne, 2003, p. 366). Smith (2003) writes that he agrees "with those who find MacIntyre's notion of practices opaque and dubious" (p. 314).

As I have argued throughout, the work of an educational psychologist is a complex interaction between the child and the psychologist, as well as a number of other factors, in which the flourishing of all is aimed at, not least of which that of the psychologist. The same can be said for the other helping professionals so that all could be termed as purposive practices (Miller, 1994, in Smith, 2003), where "purposive practices are those which, while conforming to MacIntyre's definition … nevertheless have some end beyond themselves" (Smith, 2003, p. 314). Needless to say, flourishing can also take place when failures are encountered. The work of an educational psychologist may be perceived as one which serves to impart skills and habits – as previously mentioned the psychologist can be referred cases where a particular piece of work is asked for. However, I have realised that when this happens, I enter into such situations knowing that it may be much more complex. The work of the educational psychologist is not just to conduct ability assessments, to plan and implement behavioural modification plans and other such activities, as MacIntyre's (2000) definition might imply. Educational psychology is not self-contained but has purposiveness. "Without this element of purposiveness it is difficult to see what prevents a practice from falling into self-indulgence and self-absorption, from coming in this respect to resemble an endlessly sophisticated tea-ritual" (Smith, 2003, p. 315). Besides this set of skills, there is also the process of involvement and interaction. The reason for which my involvement with Alexandra took place was simply to provide her with support in the approaching exam. However, the situation was more complex than that – it was one in which both Alexandra and I flourished through the process of working together.

MacIntyre's account of goods and virtues involves three different domains, as termed by Higgins (2003), where both receive their meaning and substance. He first explains that practices provide the space in which the virtues are exhibited. The virtues are those dispositions which will "enable us to achieve those goods which are internal to practices and the lack of which effectively prevents us from achieving any such goods" (MacIntyre, 2000, p. 191). Notwithstanding the institutional and bureaucractic difficulties, virtues are what will enable practitioners to maintain the integrity of the practice. Virtues are acquired and through their acquisition will "enable us to achieve certain goods which [MacIntyre] claims are internal to certain kinds of practices" (Nixon, 2004c, p. 118). Through the achievement of those goods, the particular dispositions which help us to achieve them are in their turn enhanced through that achievement. Carr (2006) mentions deliberation, reflection and judgement as constituents of *phronesis*, the virtue which is further explained later in this chapter. Here it suffices to point out that it is the virtue which allows the practitioner to work with dilemmas and uncertainty:

> Deliberation is necessary because, unlike *techne*, *phronesis* is not a methodical form of reasoning about how to achieve some specific end, but a deliberative process in which both means and ends are open to question. Such reasoning is reflective because the means are always modified by reflecting on the end just as an understanding of the end is always modified by reflecting on the means. And *judgement* is an essential element of *phronesis* because its outcome is a reasoned decision about what to do in a particular situation, that can be defended discursively and justified as appropriate to the circumstances in which it is being applied (Carr, 2006, p. 426).

The second domain where goods and virtues receive their meaning and substance is in relation to the good life for human beings. We experience the different virtues in our own way – with intentionality and purposefulness we provide unity and coherence of the virtues within that unity. When we achieve a good in our practice we also use it in other aspects of our lives. This would take place following the question: 'what is *my* good as a human being?' (Higgins, 2003, p. 282). Thirdly, MacIntyre sees the goods and virtues as leading to the human *telos*, and thus sees them as part of the traditions within which we practise. Thus we become good through the practice, which has to occur within the institution, but the virtues that are needed sometimes work against that institution. In fact, MacIntyre (2000) warns us not to confuse practices with institutions, which "are characteristically and necessarily concerned with … external goods" (p. 194).

In MacIntyre's definition of a practice he emphasises that we strive to achieve what is excellent and also try to go beyond it, in that from greatness in a particular practice we can learn about greatness in general. There is a further distinction between the goods internal to a practice and the standards of excellence. While the latter recede 'like the horizon as we approach it' (Higgins, 2003, p. 286), the internal goods are the journey towards that horizon. I mentioned earlier the issue of continuance – we are always in a process of becoming – by definition the *telos* outstrips our ability to reach it. We are here reminded of Standish's virtuous practitioner, who never feels that enough has been done. "But it is in the light of that *telos* that we can name the kind and degree of actual achievements made by outstanding if fallible practitioners" (Higgins, 2003, p. 286). Thus, some form of excellence "in the form of finite achievements" is possible for the practitioner who may thus deem her practice as rewarding and satisfying.

4. THE ETHICAL CHARACTER OF THE ACTIONS OF PRACTITIONERS

How can the practitioner strive towards the *telos*, the flourishing human end? How can one reach *eudaimonia*, the end that everyone aims at?

Kristjánsson (2005) explains that *phronesis*, although an intellectual virtue, serves the moral virtues in that it makes what promotes the *telos* correct. This virtue is concerned with both the universal values as well as the particular and would be the virtue involved in evaluating whether the aforementioned policies and procedures are in place for a particular case. In Alexandra's case, *phronesis* is what questioned my rigidity in following the prescribed procedure. This is very interesting as it is an intellectual virtue and yet influenced my intentions and motivations (associated with morality) to such a great extent, suggesting a greater enmeshment of the functions of a person, with less defined separations than we may suppose. "According to Aristotle the excellence of character and intelligence cannot be separated" (MacIntyre, 2000, p. 154). *Phronesis* is the ability to think about how and why one should act in order to change things, and especially to change one's life for the better. This also involves the ability to reflect upon and determine one's end which is termed *eudaimonia*. "*Phronesis*, to simplify a complex picture, is characterised by sensitivity to situated particulars and concrete cases, and by flexibility; it is the property of people of a certain character, who have relevant experience and know how to use it wisely" (Smith, 2006, p. 166–7).

> Phronesis has a double character: on the one hand it apprehends those ends which constitute human flourishing or the good for man (*Nicomachean Ethics*, 1140b 8) and on the other it involves a certain ability or cleverness which converts mere apprehension of what is to be done into the actual doing of it. For Aristotle, acting ethically is never simply a question of good intentions (though it is that); it also involves that practical intelligence or ability which converts ideas into results (Hinchliffe, 2004, p. 537).

"It is the work of *phronesis* … to coordinate the division of labour between different virtues within the individual…" (McPherson, 2005, p. 708). Thus *phronesis* has a temporal aspect to it: since it requires the practitioner's experience to be put into practice, then one must have had the time to gain such experience. Considering that the stories which are narrated in this book all took place within the first couple of years following my training, I was still quite raw in terms of such experience. However, the time which is needed is not simply that spent already as a practitioner. The time prior to the becoming of a practitioner matters as well, as this virtue needs to be taught and nurtured.

> …*phronesis* owes its inception and growth chiefly to instruction and habituation. Therefore, it is 'very important, indeed all-important' to be inculcated into the right sort of habits from youth (Aristotle, p. 35 [1103b]). For although phronesis can later be used to reconsider and revise those habits (moral dispositions) with which we were originally instilled, it will not do so unless we have been trained to appreciate the importance of such revisions. That is, although *phronesis* is an intellectual disposition, …it is, in a sense, also a

> habit which gradually kicks in through performance of the activities that the habit embodies… (Kristjánsson, 2005, p. 464).

It thus seems that this writing, through the readings and reflection of experience, has helped to increase the awareness that the moral dispositions which, perhaps, originally spurred trainees to choose to continue their studies, can now continue to influence practice through the development of wise judgement. As MacIntyre (2000) explains, it is an intellectual virtue, albeit one without which none of the virtues of character can be exercised, so that it is different from "merely a certain cunning capacity for linking means to any end rather than to those ends which are genuine goods for man" (p. 154).

As mentioned in the previous section, MacIntyre puts the idea of virtue in practice as he tentatively provides a definition: "A virtue is an acquired human quality the possession and exercise of which tends to enable us to achieve those goods which are internal to practices and the lack of which effectively prevents us from achieving any such goods" (MacIntyre, 2000, p. 191). However, it is not the case that we simply apply the virtues in our practice. Rather, the practice itself is seen as a moral source (Higgins, 2003, p. 289) and is where we encounter the good, not merely where we apply it. Thus the internal goods are the goods of the practitioners and the questions which are asked in an aretaic ethics of practising combine the particular practice with the practitioner's life in general. Thus the question 'what kind of psychologist am I becoming?' implies the question about how I should live my life, which brings together the different parts of the self nicely.

> …the liquidation of the self into a set of demarcated areas of role-playing allows no scope for the exercise of dispositions which could genuinely be accounted virtues in any sense remotely Aristotelian.… Someone who genuinely possesses a virtue can be expected to manifest it in very different types of situation, many of them situations where the practice of a virtue cannot be expected to be effective in the way that we expect a professional skill to be.… And the unity of a virtue in someone's life is intelligible only as a characteristic of a unitary life, a life that can be conceived and evaluated as a whole (MacIntyre, 2000, p. 205).

It does seem that the search for stability, which has been one of the themes in this book, can be found through this attitude, which tolerates diversity and complexity, both in others (as in the clients with whom one works) and also in the self. It may seem paradoxical, but it does seem possible to find a balance which in itself allows for imbalance, knowing that, rather than resisting contradiction, it may be better to give it its time and space. So a unitary life, one which allows for non-unitariness, is possible.

5. THE VIRTUOUS HELPING PROFESSIONAL

As I write I sometimes pull myself up short, thinking that I am being unduly hard on educational psychologists and helping professionals, and wondering just where it was that I met a psychologist who was bad, ill-intentioned and completely self-seeking, so much so that I am writing about the need of psychologists to become virtuous. Then I realise that what motivates me to write on this subject is not a result of my observing bad practice – in fact I cannot say that I have ever witnessed any. What does motivate me is the constant search for good practice, for satisfaction in fulfilling one's role, for the reaching towards *eudaimonia*. The negative aspects which I am talking about do not come from people, but emerge as part of the system which does not seem to believe in the goodness of people, and acts in such a way as to cause practitioners to feel that they are not deemed trustworthy by the institution they serve.

Thus the institution brings out guidelines for the kind of action and behaviour expected from its practitioners. Such guidelines do not however specify what kind of person the practitioner has to be. The only proviso which institutions make to ensure that a practitioner is that kind of person required for a role is to ask for a clean conduct record from the police department. Of course, in no way does an assurance that a person has never been caught doing something legally wrong mean that that person has the virtues necessary for the constant becoming of a helping professional. Through codes of ethics, through drawing up policies and procedures for prescribed action, practitioners are told how to act in certain situations when a coincidence of circumstances happens. However, virtues are not required by such documents (the fact that such documents have to be written to have any worth is itself indicative). Some codes of ethics, such as that of the British Psychological Society (2006), make reference to attitudes and judgements, and practitioners are required to develop certain character traits or dispositions which influence not so much their doing as their being. These, however, are codes of ethics which belong to the profession, not to the place where the practitioner works. In fact, Nixon when mentioning that practitioners are replacing "the traditional sense of 'belonging' to a disciplinary tradition … by a sense of 'belonging' to an institution" (2001c, p. 235), he says that the protective spaces of professionals are no longer available.

> Virtue ethics do not insist on or create homogeneity of values or exclusiveness in the profession. Rather, an ethic of virtue takes professional character as seriously as principle ethics take dilemmatic situations. But professional character is never left to its own devices, particularly in the face of a pluralistic society and the contemporary pressures of the marketplace. A professional character is a character formed and informed by the profession and one that reflects an aspiration for the ideals of that profession. The ideals of professional psychology must include conscientious decision making, but they also must include virtuous deciders, who emphasise not so much what is permitted as what is preferred Jordan and Meara (1990, p. 112).

The virtuous practitioner therefore is on a constant journey towards the fulfilment of her potential. The practitioner possesses what is necessary to reach that fulfilment, although it is never reached – MacIntyre makes the claim that the act of reaching towards that fulfilment is appreciated also for its own sake, as the internal goods of practice. Standish speaks of the virtuous person who never feels that she has done enough (2004, p. 494). The virtuous life, in fact, is only reached through the living of it - it "cannot be read off from tradition, dogma, creed or community, although each of these may provide guidance" (Nixon, 2004c, p. 117).

Standish (2005b) explores how teachers and other professionals within the education arena are stifled and demoralised so much that they withdraw. He mentions the culture of accountability and technicist trends of the education of professionals, besides the fact that "the everyday experience of work for many is beleaguered by the petty operation of power (if not by bullying), not to mention the relentless busyness that seems to have become the norm, in tandem with the expectation that one commodifies oneself in one way or another.... This can occasion some sense that one is consumed, or "eaten up" by one's work" (ibid., p. 381). Standish also gives three other factors which contribute to this stifling, and I here refer to one particular factor involving the language used. "...the way that words can go dead on us": we seem to have taken advantage of and over-used educational language and diluted its significance; moreover, we believe that by using technical language we can remove the messy unpredictability of educational practices. Standish mentions elementary school children who speak routinely of the 'criteria' which they must meet in their work – it evokes in my mind images of primary school children inappropriately dressed in very fashionable grown-up clothing.

I draw a parallel between Smith's (2006) and Standish's (2001) writing about method in the research process and the unthinking use of procedure in practice. Smith (2006, p. 160) quotes Sayer (1994) and Law (2006) as they exclaim against the replacement of the discussion of concepts and cultivation of judgement and insight with the acquisition of techniques of method. Standish (2001) points out the tendency to "cover over the ethical or to reduce it to questions of method" (p. 501). This is what I am referring to in the practice of professionals. The same is happening – practitioners find it difficult to think authentically "beyond the world-in-itself ... that the institution becomes" (Standish, 1997, p. 453). Owing to increase on demands of staff and their working hours, there is "a gradual habituation to the regime of the institution's language with its 'critical paths', 'deadlines', and its codes of initials and acronyms" (ibid.). In a review of Standish and Smith's edited book *Teaching Right and Wrong: moral education in the balance* (1997), Conroy (1998) outlines how the authors see the aforementioned habituation also in politicians and their servants as they "elide from the real complexity of moral discourse". Rather than being an obstacle to efficiency and effectiveness, the thinking of complexity is a prerequisite for doing anything meaningful and to this end, the authors call for the nurturing of Aristotelian virtues. Nixon (2001a) agrees:

> We need a language of 'telos', of imagined ends and purposes, if we are to restore professional credibility and legitimacy. What we profess is fundamental to, and informs, how we practice; how we practice is dependent upon what we profess. What we require are not new practices, but new evocations of the values underlying those practices. That is what professionalism means (p. 183).

Thus the practitioner earnestly tries to transform material into something excellent, and in doing so also transforms herself. With the *telos* which Nixon (2001a) calls for, two kinds of goods are aimed at. In the educational psychologist, the first is the excellence of the service given to children and families, unfettered by the bureaucracies and institutionalised red tape. The psychologist and the families manage to make a human connection with each other, as the vulnerabilities and potentialities of each are recognised. In doing so, the psychologist writes her own life narrative within the life of the psychologist, the second good which is still internal to practice (Higgins, 2003).

6. THE POLITICAL AND THE ETHICAL

A little more than four years have passed since this journey was started. It was noted in the beginning of this work that it is not an end product, but an opportunity for stopping and taking a look around and noting my thoughts and arguments. Having gone through this process, I find myself less frightened of and more respectful towards the complexity of my profession. I have made some way towards tolerating being uncertain. In my involvement with a particular situation where a child, parent and school require my input, I realise that my urge to 'solve' can cause me to miss out on some unexpected aspect. I have learnt to wait for this. Moreover, when the circumstances of a case seem too involved and it seems that there is nothing which can be done to support the persons, I have learnt to acknowledge this to myself. In so doing, I have the knowledge (now emerging from past experience) that I will eventually reach a plane where the level of uncertainty is one that I can work with and I am thus able to make decisions, recommend different kinds of support and also write these down in a report. The issue of writing per se was not tackled– suffice it to say that in putting something down in writing there seems to be a finality in the process, which may require a certain kind of certainty. In my reports, I have learnt that I can communicate tentatively and in so doing allow for the uncertainty – sometimes I even address it head on. Sometimes, I take the decision of communicating the uncertainty to others and have found that it was received well by others.

This is by no means easy. Fear and anxiety are still sometimes present. There is a constant search for the balance which sometimes becomes firmly tipped in one direction. The persons with whom I share these thoughts are persons I know and ones whom I believe also have this kind of disposition. They challenge me in ways which I can handle. However, I am also encouraged by the fact that those practitioners in the helping professions who have read my writing report that they resonate with it, or with some parts of it. It seems that we all struggle with the exigencies of the institutions where we work, we all struggle to keep the original reason for going into psychology alive, that of understanding people better, and helping them better as a consequence.

How is this, then, to be translated into the future of the helping professions? This was originally my doctorate thesis and was supposed to make an original contribution to Knowledge. Ironically, one of the major propositions has been a turning away from the search for knowing and towards the acceptance and toleration of not knowing. This section aims to conclude by highlighting the 'so what?'

It has been suggested that the need to know does not always emanate from the objective, rational part of ourselves, but may be the result of the unthinking need for security. Thus, an exploration of such a need and the replacement of it with a different attitude may be possible. I suggest that practitioners may allow themselves to move away from the omniscient expert role and allow for more contingency in their practice. The training of educational psychologists has now started to span over three years, which may provide more space for the formation of such professionals. Previously, the one year training course was described by many as a fast-moving express train and trainees were advised to hold on tight until the destination is reached. With the three year training course, however, the notion that the trainees are in a constant state of becoming may be suggested to the effect that this becoming is not fulfilled with the termination of the three years. Rather, the movement of balance and imbalance as practitioners are aware that living with uncertainty is possible, will continue throughout their professional life, not to mention its influence on the personal.

Thus the training of educational psychologists now has the opportunity to increase the awareness of the trainees of the virtues, and which have spurred them into wanting to work with people and children, so that these can consciously be nurtured. This was always present – I earlier argued that it is not possible to be an educational psychologist without being a moral educational psychologist. What may be different in my suggestion is that the practitioner has an increased awareness of the morality of the profession. The intellectual, the knowledge and the skills which are the tools of the educational psychologist, will thus be tempered with such virtues and emotions, thus ensuring that the clients of such practitioners will be the better for it. What is also positive is that the practitioners themselves will gain from the awareness of such practice.

> …practical philosophy is 'practical' in that it recognises that the knowledge that guides *praxis* always arises from and must always relate back to practice. And it is 'philosophical' in the sense that it seeks to raise the unreflectively acquired knowledge of the good embedded in praxis to the level of self-conscious awareness in order that practitioners may subject their pre-philosophical understanding of their practice to critical examination (Carr, 2006, p. 427).

Such practitioners are more able to see the expert in others, particularly within the clients with whom they are involved, and they are therefore more open to their voices, thus allowing unforeseen possibilities to emerge. Nietzsche (1967) writes about the 'perhaps' which may be dangerous but which may constitute the value of good and respected things. In fact, Nietzsche writes that the advent of a new order of philosophers may concern themselves with "such dangerous 'perhapses'" (p. 7), as the formulation of the new training for helping professionals may allow the idea of the practitioner who works with uncertainty. This may render the practitioner vulnerable, but in so doing may make her better able to understand and work with the vulnerabilities of others, particularly children. Through an acknowledgement of this, the practitioner works with greater sincerity and genuineness than if she represses that vulnerability and pushes towards certainty and security.

Thus, while at times in this book, the hardships of the work of an educational psychologist are bemoaned, it could be seen that such a profession is in a position of unique opportunity. The unease which educational psychologists may feel within their role allows for the virtuous practitioner, who constantly thinks how to better herself. It is not that the educational psychologist is more virtuous than any other profession, but, within the practice of the profession, there may be potential for more virtue. There may be more need for educational psychologists to be resistant under the regulatory pressures mentioned earlier in this and the previous chapters. It is up to the professionals to take advantage of such a unique opportunity and to put up resistance to what is not helpful to the clients with whom they work. The policies which were previously mentioned are put in place so that what is contingent may be regulated in universal terms. Yet, the virtuous practitioner can work with contingency and understands that living with uncertainty is not a pathology but a reflection of reality.

The virtuous practitioner allows time for circumspection, understanding that the presentation of a difficulty does not necessitate an immediate solution, contrary to expectation. Even when decisions are taken, the possibility for revision and change are still open. This does give a picture, which is rather shaky, and unstable – of course, this does not mean that one constantly flounders in indecisiveness. However, decisions should not take place at the cost of the clients with whom the practitioner is involved. Movements forward are necessary, but it is possible to conceive of and allow for inevitable setbacks.

Thus, once a practitioner is out of training, the importance of continuous professional development and supervision are immense. Here too, one must be aware of and guard against the possibility that such provisions are seen as ends in themselves. Everything that the practitioner does to keep an open attitude contributes to MacIntyre's (2000) aforementioned three different domains where goods and virtues receive their meaning and substance: the practice; in the personal self, and; for the final goal, the *telos*. Although the end is unknowable and recedes when we think we are getting close to it, it is still that towards which we reach.

> I don't feel it is necessary to know exactly what I am. The main interest in life and work is to become someone else that you were not in the beginning. If you knew when you began a book what would you say at the end, do you think that you would have the courage to write it? What is true for writing and for a love relationship is also true for life. The game is worthwhile in so far as we don't know what will be the end (Foucault in Martin, 1988, p. 9).

REFERENCES

Andrade de Azevedo, A. M. (2000). Substantive unconscious and adjective unconscious: The contribution of Wilfred Bion. *Journal of Analytical Psychology, 45*, 75–91.

Athanassoulis, N. (2004). Virtue ethics. *The Internet Encyclopaedia of Philosophy*. [Internet] Available from http://www.iep.utm.edu/v/virtue.htm [cited 2 March 2004].

Banister, P., Burman, E., Parker, I., Taylor, M., & Tindall, C. (1995). *Qualitative methods in psychology – A research guide*. UK: Open University Press.

Billig, M., et al. (1988). *Ideological dilemmas – A social psychology of everyday thinking*. London: Sage Publications.

Billington, T. (2000). *Separating, losing and excluding children: Narratives of difference*. London: Routledge Falmer.

Billington, T. (2006). *Working with children*. London: Sage.

Bion, W. R. (1970). *Attention and interpretation – A scientific approach to insight in psychoanalysis and groups*. London: Tavistock Publications.

Bion, W. R. (1994). *Learning from experience*. New Jersey, NJ: Jason Aronson, Inc.

Blake, N., Smeyers, P., Smith, R., & Standish, P. (1998). *Thinking again – Education after postmodernism*. US: Bergin and Garvey.

Brearley, M. (2002). Psychoanalysis and the body-mind problem. *Ratio*, 429–443.

Buchanan, I. (2005). Space in the age of non-place. In I. Buchanan & G. Lambert (Eds.), *Deleuze and space*. Edinburgh: Edinburgh University Press.

Carr, W. (1983). Can educational research be scientific? *Journal of Philosophy of Education, 17*(1), 35–43.

Carr, W. (2006). Philosophy, methodology and action research. *Journal of Philosophy of Education, 40*(4), 421–435.

Carrington, G., Griffin, D., Hollis, I., & Parry, J. (2002). Ethical problem-solving in the practice of educational psychology. *Educational and Child Psychology, 19*(1), 30–45.

Cook, M. (2003). About 'After Virtue' by A. MacIntyre. [Internet] Available from http://blogs.salon.com/0002889/stories/2003/10/05/aboutaftervirtueByAMacintyre.html [cited 2 March 2004].

Conroy, J. C. (1998). Review of teaching right and wrong: Moral education in the balance. *Journal of Moral Education, 27*(2), 252–255.

Da Silva, G. (1997). *The emergence of thinking: Bion as the link between Freud and the Neurosciences*. [Internet] Available from http://www.sicap.it/~merciai/bion/papers/silva.htm [cited 19 November 2004]

Damasio, A. (1999). *The feeling of what happens: Body, emotion and the making of consciousness*. London: Vintage Press.

Damasio, A. (2004). *Looking for Spinoza*. London: Vintage Press.

Deleuze, G., & Guattari, F. (1987). *A thousand plateaus: Capitalism and schizophrenia*. London: The Athelone Press Ltd.

Derrida, J. (1992). Force of law: The "mystical foundation of authority". In D. Carlson, D. Cornell & M. Rosenfeld (Eds.), *Deconstruction and the possibility of justice*. London: Routledge.

Dunne, J. (2003). Arguing for teaching as a practice: A reply to Alasdair MacIntyre. *Journal of Philosophy of Education, 37*(2), 353–369.

Durkheim, E. (1984). *The division of labour in society*. London: Macmillan Press.

Egan, G. (1994). *The skilled helper*. California, CA: Brooks/Cole Publishing Company.

Elliott, C. D. (1990). *Differential ability scales: Administration and scoring manual*. New York: Harcourt Brace Jovanovich, Inc.

EPNET The Educational Psychology List. (2005). Email discussion list [mailto: epnet@jiscmail.ac.uk]. [cited 24–25 August 2005].

Feyerabend, P. (1975). Against method. *Wikipedia*. [Internet] Available from http://en.wikipedia.org/wiki/Paul_Feyerabend [cited 17 January 2006].

Field, J. (1990). *A life of own's own*. London: Virago Press Ltd.

REFERENCES

Francis, R. D. (2002). The need for a professional ethic. *Educational and Child Psychology, 19*(1), 7–15.

Franey, J. (2002). Ethical mindfulness and professional development in local educational authority psychology services. *Educational and Child Psychology, 19*(1), 16–29.

Gersch, I. S. (2004). Educational psychology – In an age of uncertainty. *The Psychologist, 8*(3), 142–145.

Gilligan, C. (1993). *In a different voice: Psychological theory and women's development.* Massachusetts, MA: Harvard University Press.

Goodwin, D., Pope, C., Mort, M., & Smith, A. (2003). Ethics and ethnography: An experiential account. *Qualitative Health Research, 13*(4), 567–577.

Higgins, C. (2003). MacIntyre's moral theory and the possibility of an aretaic ethics of teaching. *Journal of Philosophy of Education, 37*(2), 279–292.

Hinchcliffe, G. (2004). Work and human flourishing. *Educational Philosophy and Theory, 36*(5), 535–547.

Hinshelwood, R. D. (1998). *Clinical Klein.* London: Free Association Books.

Hollway, W. (1994). *Subjectivity and method in psychology.* London: Sage Publications.

Hollway, W., & Jefferson, T. (2001). *Doing qualitative research differently.* London: Sage Publications.

Horne, M., Sowa, A., & Isenman, D. (2000). Philosophical assumptions in Freud, Jung and Bion: Questions of causality. *Journal of Analytical Psychology, 45*, 109–121.

Hunt, C. (2001). Shifting shadows: Metaphors and maps for facilitating reflective practice. *Reflective Practice, 2*(3), 275–287.

Hyatt, D. (2006). Affordances of empowerment: A pedagogical analytical and heuristic tool for textual and discoursal uncloaking. *Quaderns de Filologia. Estudis Lungistics, XI*, 1–12.

Jordan, A. E., & Meara, N. M. (1990). Ethics and the professional practice of psychologists: The role of virtues and principles. *Professional Psychology: Research and Practice, 21*(2), 107–114.

Katayama, K. (2003). Is the virtue approach to moral education viable in a plural society? *Journal of Philosophy of Education, 37*(2), 325–338.

Kaufman, W. (1989) Existentialism is a humanism. *Existentialism from Dostoyevsky to Sartre.* [Internet] Available from http://www.marxists.org/reference/archive/sartre/works/exist/sartre.htm [cited: 2 December 2005].

Kitchener, K. S. (1996). Professional codes of ethics and ongoing moral problems in psychology. In W. O'Donohue & R. F. Kitchener (Eds.), *The philosophy of psychology.* London: Sage Publications.

Klein, M. (1997). *Envy and gratitude and other works 1946–1963.* London: Vintage.

Kohlberg, L. (1979). *Measuring moral judgement.* Worcester, MA: Clark University Press.

Kristjánsson, K. (2005). Smoothing it: Some Aristotelian misgivings about the phronesis-praxis perspective open education. *Educational Philosophy and Theory, 37*(4), 455–473.

Law, J. (2006). *After method – Mess in social science research.* London: Routledge.

Levering, B. (2006). Epistemological issues in phenomenological research: How authoritative are people's accounts of their own perceptions? *Journal of Philosophy of Education, 40*(4), 451–462.

Lindsay, G., & Colley, G. (1995). Values, ethics and psychology. *The Psychologist, 8*, 493–498.

Lindsay, G. (1999). Ethical dilemmas of psychotherapists. *The Psychologist, 12*(4), 182–185.

Lyotard, J. (1979). *The postmodern condition – A report on knowledge.* [Internet] Available from http://www.marxists.org/reference/subject/philosophy/works/fr/lyotard.htm [cited 3 August 2006].

McAuliffe, D., & Sudbery, J. (2005). 'Who do I tell?' Support and consultation in cases of ethical conflict. *Journal of Social Work, 5*(1), 21–43.

McNab, I. (2001). A personal submission to the working group on the future role and training of educational psychologists (EPWG).

McNab, I. (2005). *Relationship networks and the concept of 'the client', Staffordshire County Council.* Educational Psychology Service.

McNamee, M. (2001). The guilt of whistle-blowing: Conflicts in action research and educational ethnography. *Journal of Philosophy of Education, 35*(3), 423–441.

McPherson, I. (2005). Reflexive learning: Stages towards wisdom with Dreyfus. *Educational Philosophy and Theory, 37*(5), 705–718.

MacIntyre, A. (2000). *After virtue: A study in moral theory* (2nd ed.). London: Gerald Duckworth and Co. Ltd.

MacIntyre, A. (1999). *Dependent rational animals.* London: Duckworth and Co. Ltd.
MacIntyre, A., & Dunne, J. (2002). Alasdair MacIntyre on education: In dialogue with Joseph Dunne. *Journal of Philosophy of Education, 36*(1), 1–19.
Martin, L. H., et al. (1988). *Technologies of the self: A seminar with Michel Foucault* (pp. 9–15). London: Tavistock.
Meilaender, G. (1999). Dependent rational animals: Why human beings need the virtues and the MacIntyre reader. *First Things, 96*, 47–55.
Medawar, P. (1967). *The art of the soluble.* London: Methuen and Co Ltd.
Mellor, N. (1998). Notes from a method. *Educational Action Research, 6*(3), 453–470.
Mellor, N. (2001). Messy method: The unfolding story. *Educational Action Research, 9*(3), 465–484.
Mercieca, D. (2003). *Report on Gemma.*
Mercieca, D. (2004). *What kind of psychologist am I to become?* Paper presented for M.Phil – Ph.D. conversion viva.
Mercieca, D. (September 2002 to June 2006). *Journal (Personal).*
Midgley, M. (1992). *Science as salvation – A modern myth and its meaning.* London: Routledge.
Ministry of Education, Youth and Employment. (2005, June). *For all children to succeed: A new network organisation for quality education in Malta.* Malta.
Ministry for Education, Youth and Employment. (2005, June). *Inclusive and special education review.* Malta.
Morstyn, R. (2002). The therapist's dilemma: Be sincere or fake it? *Australasian Psychiatry, 10*(4), 325–329.
Nagel, T. (2002). *Mortal questions.* Cambridge: Cambridge University Press.
Nietzsche, F. (1967). *Beyond good and evil – Prelude to a philosophy of the future.* London: George Allen and Unwin Ltd.
Nixon, J. (2001a). 'Not without dust and heat': The moral bases of the 'new' academic professionalism. *British Journal of Educational Studies, 49*(2), 173–186.
Nixon, J. (2001b). Imagining ourselves into being: Conversing with Hannah Arendt. *Pedagogy, Culture and Society, 9*(2), 221–236.
Nixon, J. (2001c). Towards a new academic professionalism: A manifesto of hope. *British Journal of Sociology of Education, 22*(2), 287–244.
Nixon, J. (2003). Professional renewal as a condition of institutional change: Rethinking academic work. *International Studies on Sociology of Education, 13*(1), 3–15.
Nixon, J. (2004a). What is theory? *Educar, 34*, 27–37.
Nixon, J. (2004b). Education for the good society: The integrity of academic practice. *London Review of Education, 2*(3), 245–252.
Nixon, J. (2004c). Learning the language of deliberative democracy. In J. Nixon & M. Walker (Eds.), 2004. *Reclaiming universities from a runaway world.* Berkshire: Open University Press.
Nixon, J., Marks, A., Rowland, S., & Walker, M. (2001). Towards a new academic professionalism: A manifesto of hope. *British Journal of Sociology of Education, 22*(2), 227–244.
Nixon, J., Martin, J., McKeown, P., & Ranson, S. (1997). Towards a learning profession: Changing codes of occupational practice within the new management of education. *British Journal of Sociology of Education, 18*(1), 5–28.
Norwich, B. (2005). Future direction for professional educational psychology. *School Psychology International, 26*(4), 387–397.
Oakes, E. T. (1996). The achievement of Alasdair MacIntyre. *First Things, 65*, 22–26.
Parker, I., Georgaca, E., Harper, D., McLaughlin, T., & Stowell-Smith, M. (1995). *Deconstructing psychopathology.* London: Sage Publications.
Parker, I. (2005). *Qualitative psychology – Introducing radical research.* Berkshire: Open University Press.
Pring, R. (2000). The 'false dualism' of educational research. *Journal of Philosophy of Education, 34*(2), 247–260.
Pring, R. (2001). The virtues and vices of an educational researcher. *Journal of Philosophy of Education, 35*(3), 407–421.

Rogers, C. (2001). *A therapist's view of psychotherapy – On becoming a person.* London: Constable.
Rorty, R. (1989). *Contingency, irony and solidarity.* Cambridge: Cambridge University Press.
Rowbottom, D. P., & Aiston, S. (2006). The myth of 'scientific method' in contemporary educational research. *Journal of Philosophy of Education, 40*(2), 138–156.
Rowe, M., Frey, J., Bailey, M., Fisk, P., & Davidson, L. (2001). Clinical responsibility and client autonomy: Dilemmas in mental health work at the margins. *American Journal of Orthopsychiatry, 71*(4), 400–407.
Sandler, P. C. (1997). The apprehension of psychic reality: Extensions of Bion's theory of alpha-funtion. *Journal of Psycho-Analysis, 78,* 43–52.
Schön, D. A. (2000). *The reflective practitioner - How professionals think in action.* Aldershot: Arena-Ashgate Publishing Limited.
Segal, J. (2004). *Melanie Klein* (2nd ed.). London: Sage Publications Limited.
Skoe E. E. A., Eisenberg, N., & Cumberland, A. (2002). The role of reported emotion in real-life and hypothetical moral dilemmas. *Personality and Social Psychology Bulletin, 28*(7), 962–973.
Small, R. (2001). Codes are not enough: What philosophy can contribute to the ethics of educational research. *Journal of Philosophy of Education, 35*(3), 387–406.
Smeyers, P. (2001). Qualitative versus quantitative research design: A plea for paradigmatic tolerance in educational research. *Journal of Philosophy of Education, 35*(3), 477–495.
Smith, A. (1776). An inquiry into the nature and causes of the wealth of nations. [Internet] Available from http://www.adamsmith.org/smith/won-b1-c1.htm [cited 11 November 2006].
Smith, R. (2003). Thinking with each other: The peculiar practice of the university. *Journal of Philosophy of Education, 37*(2), 309–323.
Smith, R. (2006). As if by machinery: The levelling of educational research. *Journal of Philosophy of Education, 40*(2), 157–168.
Smith, J. A., & Smith, A. H. (2001). Dual relationships and professional integrity: An ethical dilemma case of a family counselor as clergy. *The Family Journal: Counseling and Therapy for Couples and Families, 9*(4), 438–443.
Soja, E. W. (1998). *Thirdspace – Journeys to Los Angeles and other real-and-imagined places.* Oxford: Blackwell.
Spinoza, B. (1989). *Ethics.* London: J.M. Demt and Sons.
Standish, P. (1997). Heidegger and the technology of further education. *Journal of Philosophy of Education, 31*(3), 439–459.
Standish, P. (2001). Data return: The sense of the given in educational research. *Journal of Philosophy of Education, 35*(3), 497–518.
Standish, P. (2002a). Editorial. *Journal of Philosophy of Education, 36*(1).
Standish, P. (2002b). Disciplining the profession: Subjects subject to procedure. *Educational Philosophy and Theory, 35*(1), 5–23.
Standish, P. (2002c). Editorial. *Journal of Philosophy of Education, 36*(4).
Standish, P. (2003). Editorial. *Journal of Philosophy of Education, 37*(3).
Standish, P. (2004). Europe, continental philosophy and the philosophy of education. *Comparative Education, 40*(4), 485–501.
Standish, P. (2005a). Towards an economy of higher education. *Critical Quarterly, 47*(1–2), 53–71.
Standish, P. (2005b). Democratic participation and the body politic. *Educational Theory, 55*(4), 371–384.
Symington, J., & Symington, N. (2004). *The clinical thinking of Wilfred Bion.* East Sussex: Brunner-Routledge.
The British Psychological Society. (2006). *Codes of ethics and conduct.*
Tickle, L. (2001). Opening windows, closing doors: Ethical dilemmas in educational action research. *Journal of Philosophy of Education, 35*(3), 346–359.
Tolman, C. (1994). *Psychology, society and subjectivity – An introduction to German critical psychology.* London: Routledge.
Walter, J. L., & Peller, J. E. (1992). *Becoming solution-focused in brief therapy.* US: Brunnel/Mazel.
Warner Brothers. (1999). *The matrix.* [DVD]. New York: Warner Brothers.

Webster, A., & Bond, T. (2002). Structuring uncertainty: Developing an ethical framework for professional practice in educational psychology. *Educational and Child Psychology, 19*(1), 16–29.

Webster, A., & Lunt, I. (2002). Ethics, professionalisation and the future landscape of educational psychology. *Educational and Child Psychology, 19*(1), 16–29.

Wellington, J. (2000). *Educational Research – Contemporary issues and practical approaches.* London: Continuum.

Williams, R. (1976). *Keywords – A vocabulary of culture and society*. London: Fontana Press.

Winch, P. (1990). *The idea of a social science and its relation to philosophy* (2nd ed.). London: Routledge.